h0129963080

handmade
halloween

ideas for a happy, haunted celebration

Country Living

handmade
halloween

ideas for a happy, haunted celebration

text by Zazel Lovén

photography by Keith Scott Morton

styling by Amy Leonard

foreword by Nancy Mernit Soriano

HEARST BOOKS
NEW YORK

It is the policy of William Morrow and Company, Inc., and its imprints and affiliates, recognizing the importance of preserving what has been written, to print the books we publish on acid-free paper, and we exert our best efforts to that end.

Library of Congress Cataloging-in-Publication Data
Country living handmade Halloween : ideas for a happy, haunted celebration.
        p.   cm.
    Includes index.
    ISBN 0-688-16775-6
    1. Halloween decorations.   2 Handicraft.   I. Country living (New York, N.Y.)
    TT900.H32C68   1999
    745.594'1--dc21   99-23394
                                                                                              CIP

Printed in Singapore

First Edition
10 9 8 7 6 5 4 3 2 1

Text set in Galliard

For Country Living
Nancy Mernit Soriano, Editor-in-Chief
John Mack Carter, President, Hearst Magazine Enterprises

Photos on pages 1, 6, and 8 styled by the editors of Country Living

www.williammorrow.com
www.countryliving.com

Produced by Smallwood & Stewart, Inc., New York City

Art Director ● Debbie Sfetsios
Designer ● Alexandra Maldonado
Editor ● Carrie Chase

table of contents

foreword

I love Halloween—just as much as when I was a child. I can remember the challenge of coming up with the most creative costume, the fun of parading from house to house to amass the largest bag of treats, and the excitement of planning the perfect party with friends. Today, I continue to enjoy the spirit of Halloween and take every opportunity to make it a special day for my own child.

Halloween is one of those rare occasions when we can let our imaginations run wild. For one day, we can become anything our heart desires—a fairy princess or a cowboy. We can test our skills at carving scary or comical faces in pumpkins. And, we can transform a normal interior into a haunted house, complete with fake cobwebs, wispy ghosts, and unexpected surprises.

In this book, we offer page after page of fun projects and suggestions for celebrating this special holiday. Chapter One details projects for observing the day in the proper spirit—from decorating your front door to throwing a Halloween party. Chapter Two is devoted to pumpkin-carving—an undertaking that has moved into an art form of sorts. And Chapter Three offers costume and trick-or-treat ideas to inspire and guarantee a night of fun for everyone.

— Nancy Mernit Soriano, Editor-in-Chief

introduction

When children gather outside a spooky house, clutching large candy-filled bags in their little hands and swathed in costumes, they are taking part in a tradition that dates back more than two thousand years. Bats, witches, fires on a dark night—the images we associate with Halloween have been a part of harvest celebrations from the days when people believed that the world was overrun with spirits and demons, and that magic held sway over man. According to the pre-Christian Celtic calendar, the beginning of winter— the period when the darkest forces of nature ruled—fell on October 31. This was when the Celts celebrated the completion of the harvest and the beginning of a new year. They lit bonfires to give the sun strength through the winter months to come, and they observed the feast day of Samhain, the lord of the dead. The Celts believed the spirits of those who had left this earth during the past year roamed about at this time, looking for a final resting place. They would try to placate the wandering souls with gifts of food or, conversely, chase them away by lighting bonfires. They wore frightening disguises so the dead souls would pass them by, and some of the masked villagers would form a parade, to trick spirits into following them out of town.

After the Celts were conquered by the Romans, around the time of the birth of Christ, their rituals and beliefs were incorporated into Roman observations, including the festival of Pomona held on November 1. On her feast day, the Romans thanked their goddess of fruits and gardens for a good harvest by playing games, running races, and setting out apples and nuts in her honor.

As Christianity spread throughout Europe, early church leaders wisely decided not to discourage the pagan rituals associated with the beginning of winter, and instead incorporated them into the emerging religion. The Celtic Samhain feast day became the Feast of All Saints, and the night before was called All Hallows' Eve (a hallow is the spirit of a dead person or saint). Over the years the night became known as Halloween. Bonfires and masquerading were encouraged, not to frighten the wandering dead as before, but to honor early Christian saints and the souls of the recently departed. (The fires also served nicely to keep the devil away.) Visiting neighbors on All Hallows' Eve was also promoted by the church, giving early sanction to trick or treating.

Eventually the rituals of this pagan-Christian celebration were brought to the United States. The Puritans did not celebrate Halloween, although the tradition of honoring the dead on All Saints' Day, or Hallowmas, was sanctioned by the church in Virginia. Later colonists, more superstitious, would gather together on the night of October 31, believing that to be in the company of others would lessen the chances of running into the spirits of the dead. The celebration of the harvest also brought people together in late fall, when they rejoiced over the bounty, bobbed for apples, and told ghost stories. But it was the Irish immigrants who embedded Halloween in American life. As the Irish fanned out across the country, they carried their combination of ancient Celtic folk beliefs and religious celebrations with them. Games of divination, carrying a lit turnip on nocturnal visits from house to house, and parading in costume all were a part of the Irish way of celebrating Halloween. With the acceptance of these rituals by the general population, Halloween became a firmly rooted American tradition, and the jack-o'-lantern (now made from the New World pumpkin instead of the European turnip) became the official symbol of Autumn's scariest night.

chapter one

it's halloween!

On Halloween night, spirits wander as ghosts and goblins, children roam the neighborhood in **costumes and masks**, houses are done up in all sorts of scary ways, jack-o'-lanterns light the way, and treats are handed out as prevention against naughty pranks. Halloween is indeed a time to let your **imagination** run wild. It's a night for fun, a night for transformations. Change who you are by putting on a costume. Transform a humble pumpkin into a light-filled goblin. Disguise your home as a scary **haunted** house or simply make it a place to welcome the little monsters who will spare you a trick if you hand out a treat.

Today Halloween is celebrated largely as a joyous, **frightful** occasion for the kids, but it gives grown-ups an excuse to let down their hair as well. The holiday has also become an opportunity for families to spend time doing **creative** things together. Making costumes and decorations, carving pumpkins, planning for trick-or-treaters—these activities are enjoyed by both children and adults. You don't have to believe in ghosts and goblins to observe—and create anew—the traditions of the **scariest** night of the year!

haunted home

When it comes to decorating for Halloween, whether for a grand party or for simply scaring the neighborhood goblins, look to the icons of the holiday for inspiration. Their simple shapes are instantly recognizable: a carved pumpkin, a witch on a broom, a black cat, a flying bat, a giant spider. These are the stuff of costumes, cut-outs for windows, party invitations, even cookies. To set the stage for your Halloween house, start with the jack-o'-lantern, the most enduring Halloween symbol of all and the beacon that guides trick-or-treaters to the house where a welcome is waiting.

The traditional produce of fall can be a large part of decorating for Halloween, whether you live in a city or miles from civilization. Indian corn, gourds, pumpkins, and other fall vegetables from a farmers' market are so evocative that they can become a simple, beautiful centerpiece, mantelpiece display, or porch still-life with little or no adornment. Sheaves of cornstalks attached to fence posts, porch railings, and house pillars, though today seen as merely decorative, actually represent the coming of winter and all that Halloween originally stood for. Consider these other ideas for bringing Halloween atmosphere to your home:

- Create an arrangement of hollowed-out crown-of-thorn squash and bottleneck gourds to hold candles.
- Cornhusks and branches with autumn leaves and berries or dangling apples celebrate the harvest season and are fetching hung at doorways, room entrances, and around mantels.
- Moss, spread out with fall-colored leaves, makes a fitting centerpiece on a serving table. Hollowed-out cabbages, pumpkins, and turnips are fun vessels for Halloween treats.
- Arrange tall bare branches in pots strategically placed around the room—they'll look like spooky "skeleton hands" reaching out.
- Fake spider webs make everything appear musty and old. For instant creepiness, pull them around bare tree branches, a musty thrift shop portrait in a distressed frame, or a junk shop candelabra.
- Glue-gun fall leaves, or cutouts of ghosts, skeletons, and witches, onto sheer black fabric and hang in a doorway to create a dramatic entrance to a haunted room.
- And that old-fashioned broom in the corner—was it left by a guest, or . . . ?

The most exciting thing about fixing up a house for Halloween is that so many ideas can be executed with things found around the yard and house (be sure to look in the basement, garage, and attic). Leaves, branches, and a rake; clothes from an old chest in the attic; cardboard boxes, tin cans, and broom sticks—all can add to your Halloween decorating plans. Even a haunted house can be created with everyday things from the pantry (think cold cooked spaghetti, globs of gelatin). Once the lights are dimmed, people's imaginations go a long way.

Outside, don't make it too easy for little goblins to demand their treats: Create a mystery by illuminating the pathway to the house with a ghostly glow—small carved pumpkins or paper bags block-printed with Halloween figures, all giving off flickering candle light. Or turn the yard into a creepy setup for whatever waits on the other side of the door: A well-situated tree is just where ghosts like to hang out. If there's not a convenient tree, drape a white sheet over a pumpkin set atop two bales of hay. Sheets or large white pieces of construction paper cut in ghostly shapes and tacked over windows will fill all who approach with apprehension, especially when the only light inside comes from a candle (not too close to sheets or paper, please).

Creating a house of horrors is a wonderful opportunity to let the trickster side of your decorating imagination fly. A few special effects in a darkened room are simple to concoct. But keep in mind that young children scare easily and on Halloween they are especially susceptible—it is best to set an age limit, as the noises and surprises might be too frightening for smaller children. Plan on the walk-through taking only a minute or two, and pick a spot that is easy to enter and exit. Ask kids and friends to share the work; the more ideas and the more people to carry them out, the more creative the results. And try some of the suggestions on the following pages.

scary films

Show these classic movies at holiday time to set the Halloween mood:

The Black Castle 1952

The Black Cat 1934

Dr. Jekyll and Mr. Hyde 1920

The Exorcist 1973

Fall of the House of Usher 1960

Freaks 1932

The Haunting 1963

The Lost Boys 1987

Nosferatu 1922

Phantom of the Opera 1925

The Pit and the Pendulum 1961

The Raven 1935

Rosemary's Baby 1968

The Shining 1980

creating a haunted house

Jana Hyten first created a haunted house for the ghostly guests attending her daughter's Halloween party. Word about it spread, and neighborhood trick-or-treaters started stopping by. Now, every Halloween at dusk, children line up outside the Hyten house. In small groups they are escorted through the scary rooms—two minutes of scream-inducing sights. As they leave a sweet reward awaits: Each child dips a hand into a black caldron filled with candy. Here are some tips and ideas from Jana (many of which will work for party decorating, as well):

● First impressions set the stage: In the yard or up a walkway, stick picnic torches spray-painted black in the ground and place a lighted candle in each.

● Make a graveyard in the front yard by cutting tombstones out of foamboard bought at an art supply store. Spray-paint the foamboard gray and add dabs of green paint for age. Think up funny names, like Al B. Seenyu, Ima Goast, R. U. Scared, and paint them in black.

● Cut large silhouettes of menacing figures or ghosts out of black poster board. Hang in windows with string or tape. Light from behind for best effect.

● Hang black fabric at the entrance to the haunted rooms.

● Tilt pictures on walls at odd angles (look for old "instant ancestor" portraits in junk stores or at yard sales, the more severe and scary the expressions, the better!).

● To heighten the mood, play a homemade tape of creepy noises: a door creaking, chains on the floors, an owl screeching, a scream, the cackle of a witch, water dripping on tin.

● Take dead tree branches and pull spider webbing (available from Halloween and party supply stores) from branch to branch; place rubber spiders and large bats cut from black construction paper in the webbing. For more atmosphere: drape sphagnum moss (from florist supply shops) from branches.

● Scatter dead, wilted flower arrangements around the house.

● Replace bulbs in lamps with flicker bulbs, and use artists' clip-on lamps covered with colored gels (red, green, and blue all give off an eerie light) to cast scary shadows.

● Weave a massive spider web in a doorway by taping rope across the top and tying dozens of pieces of long thread to it. Let the thread hang down to a couple of feet above the floor. As children pass through the doorway, the threads will feel like creepy spider webs.

● Use a projector to project spooky slides or shadows onto the ceiling or walls of a darkened room.

● For a mad scientist's lab, place around the room, on shelves, or above doors old bottles filled with colored water, old books, old clocks, or old rusty tools such as hatchets and saw blades (these should be out of reach of small hands). Pull spider webbing very thinly around the props.

● Clear most of the furniture from a room and cover the remaining pieces with the inexpensive black fabric used for lining clothing. Shred with a single-edged razor and cut hems unevenly to give the appearance of age.

● Recruit friends to play Dracula and Severed Head. Dracula wears a black cape and white makeup (don't forget the red drops of blood!) and lies in a cardboard box (from a large appliance) painted black. He only stirs when a group of party-goers passes. For Severed Head, use a table with removable leaves. Replace one leaf with heavy corrugated cardboard that has a head-size hole in its center. Cover the table with black,

shredded lining material—long enough to hide an adult crouching beneath the table. Cut a head-size hole in a large round plastic tray (available at a party supply store). Scatter old lettuce leaves, rubber rats, and bugs around the table. Add to the surprise by covering the head with a large domed lid (try a kitchen supply store). As children pass by, an adult lifts the lid, revealing Severed Head, complete with white face paint and red lipstick around its neck.

● Gather old bowls and small pails for "Guess the Body Part." Try these out:

HAIR • wet yarn

EARS • dried fruit

NOSES • small pickles

ARMS • dog bones

INSIDES • wet yarn or undercooked macaroni or spaghetti

EYEBALLS • olives or peeled grapes

TEETH • broken bits of chalk

FINGERS • string beans

BRAINS • small wet sponges or pieces of cauliflower

party ideas

Children and adults alike delight in donning costumes and celebrating Halloween. Plan a party with a come-as-whom-you-*want*-to-be theme, and let the ages of your guests determine the decorating scheme and activities. And be sure to keep the hungry hordes fed—see the recipes beginning on page 93 for suggestions.

CHILDREN'S PARTY

Throw a kids' party in lieu of trick-or-treating or to continue the fun after everyone has made the rounds of the neighborhood. Come up with cute party favors: pencils embellished with pumpkins made from small Styrofoam balls painted orange; miniature pumpkins that the kids can decorate with pens or paints as part of the party; or paper-bag pumpkins, made by stuffing a brown paper bag with newspaper, twisting the top to create a stem, and painting on a jack-o'-lantern face.

Decorate the party room with Halloween icons: Spiders, jack-o'-lanterns, black cats, flying bats, witches, and owls are all simple shapes. Children can help to make much of what goes into creating the right atmosphere. To start, make stencils of each shape from heavy cardboard. Let the children trace the shapes onto black construction paper, then cut them out and hang by pieces of black or white thread from windows and doorways. Make a witch mobile for the center of the room: Bend a hanger into a circle and, using black thread, tie on three witches on brooms cut from black construction paper, and a crescent moon cut from orange paper. Using black yarn, tape or tie the hanger to the ceiling or a lighting fixture. (Remember to keep the lights low—this party room shouldn't be too bright!)

Simple noisemakers are one way to scare ghosts and keep them from crashing a party. Have the kids make ghost chasers: Cover tin cans in orange or black paper and poke a stick through a plastic lid fitted onto the can opening; fill with dried beans or gravel. Or tape together two tinfoil plates painted with fright faces and fill with uncooked rice. They'll make lots of noise when children shake them.

Yucky Yummies

Black, orange, and/or yucky is the finger food of choice at a children's Halloween party.
- Black and orange jelly beans layered into mason jars are pretty to the eye and can be given as favors at the end of the night.
- A sweet pumpkin bread (baking will make it dark) and chunks of cheddar cheese will appeal to many children.
- Hollow out good-sized oranges by cutting

off the tops and scooping out the insides with a serrated-edge grapefruit spoon. With a felt-tipped pen, draw a jack-o'-lantern face on each orange. Fill with squares of red Jell-O, bits of the orange segments, and cantaloupe chunks. Tell the little party guests that each head is filled with brains.

- For thirsty revelers, whip up Dracula's favorite, a "blood" milkshake: In a blender, combine vanilla yogurt, frozen strawberries or raspberries, and a few ice cubes. Or blend cranberry and orange juice with a dollop of raspberry sherbet. For creepier slurps, make vampire-eyeball ice cubes. The day before the party, pour cranberry juice half way into ice cube trays. Freeze until the juice is slush, then stick a green grape in the middle and put back in the freezer. Pop one in each drink.

- Too much "clean" stuff is a bad idea, so be sure to include a tray of dirt and worms fresh from the graveyard. Bake crumbly brownies or dark chocolate cookies. Break into bite-sized pieces, mix with gummy worms, and garnish with lots of crumbs!

Spooky Games and Activities

Children like to be scared, but not too scared. Start them off gently, with a project that requires concentration and creativity. Brown paper bags (painted black or white ahead of time if you wish), or white paper plates with string attached for tying around a small head, are quick and easy masks. Cut two holes for eyes, and set up an assortment of poster paints, crayons, or markers—whatever is best for the age group—to let the children express themselves.

Later in the party, add the thrills. A simple haunted castle is easy to create, especially if you recruit older children to help (those who like to act will quickly volunteer!). If the party is in the afternoon, cover windows with dark paper. Use flashlights or out-of-reach candles to cast a spooky glow. In one corner, have a witch cackling while stirring a cauldron (a big, round basket covered with black crepe paper and with crinkled red paper at the bottom of the pot, for fire, and a broom for stirring). Next stop is the goblin's graveyard. For the gravestones, spray-paint large grocery bags gray, write "scary" sayings (like Here Today, Gone Tomorrow) on them in squiggly letters with a black marker, and stuff with newspaper. Hang construction-paper bats and white balloons with faces from the ceiling. Drag an old armchair into the scene and drape with black fabric, then cover a willing participant with a sheet and set him down in the chair. The ghost can admonish the visitors to creep along quietly so they don't wake the dead. Last stop is the vampire hideaway. Have Dracula stand behind a table covered with black cloth or paper. Hang large black spiders behind him, and line up empty glass jars of varying sizes. Fill with colored water, red paint for blood, or with shaving cream spilling out.

Games should be a big part of the party. Bobbing for apples has been part of Halloween celebrations for a long time. All but the youngest children can participate. Fill a large galvanized tub with water. Tie a sheet, or something protective, around the neck of each contestant. Each child kneels by the tub and tries to grab an apple using teeth only (blindfolding is optional).

● A fortune-telling game that dates back to the pioneer days is called Three Luggies. Place three large bowls on a table. In one put an apple, the second a nut, and in the third put dirt. Blindfold the player, shift around the bowls, turn the player around twice, and have her reach into a bowl. An apple represents good luck, a nut means things will remain the same, and dirt indicates troubles ahead.

● Fill a room with orange and black balloons. The goal is to cross the room without breaking any of the balloons—the challenge is that each participant is blindfolded!

● Make Halloween finger puppets and have the children (or older siblings) make up stories.

● Create a list of all the words associated with Halloween (the children can shout them out)

and then write poems using the words.

● Weather-permitting, have a pumpkin hunt outside. Hide miniature pumpkins, and have the children search until each one has found a pumpkin. If the children are older, a scavenger hunt is more challenging.

● Making a tape of Halloween noises is fun, and the tape can then be used for a haunted castle. Each child can make a noise into the tape recorder. Suggest shrieking, moaning and groaning, thunder (rattle a sheet of poster board), fire (crinkle a cellophane bag), evil laughing, chains clanging, wind howling, footsteps clomping, an owl hooting, a wolf howling, a witch cackling, a door opening, a ghost laughing, a cat meowing. Drawing a picture or writing a poem while listening to the tape is fun for older children.

● Wrap-the-Mummy sounds like it couldn't be messier, though it is guaranteed to top a child's list of favorite party activities. Pair children off so that one is the mummy and the other is the mummy wrapper. Each pair gets a roll of white toilet paper with instructions to "wrap the mummy!" After one mummy is wrapped, it's then the turn of the partner to "wrap the mummy."

● For young children, pin-the-spider-on-the-spider-web is a natural substitute for the time-honored donkey favorite.

GHOSTLY GROWN-UP GATHERING

While still considered mostly a children's holiday, each year more and more adults are getting into the Halloween fun. What better way to keep those evil spirits at bay than by throwing a party! Selecting the right space will go a long way towards creating a spine-tingling ambiance. There's atmosphere galore in a musty basement, garage, or old barn.

If the weather is too cold for these spooky settings, it's not hard to turn your house into a haunted one. For a highly dramatic entrance, do as the Victorians did and let fire shed the only light, with jack-o'-lanterns by the door, a fire in the fireplace, and candles everywhere.

Set the fun tone for a grown-up Halloween party, beginning with the invitations. Handmade invites can be attached to miniature pumpkins and left on doorsteps. Give your party a name: Revive a pioneer tradition and call Halloween night Snap Apple Night or Nutcrack Night, so named because the games and party food revolved around newly harvested apples and nuts.

Stock up on merchandise such as small lights in the shapes of skulls and bats, available seasonally in lighting stores. Set up a bar with seasonal favorites such as cider, lager, black

scary books

Washington Irving's *The Legend of Sleepy Hollow* is the quintessential American ghost story and can be found in many anthologies, including the first one listed below:

The Sketchbook, by Washington Irving (Signet Press)

12 Classic Ghost Stories by Wilkie Collins, M. R. James, Charles Dickens, and Others, edited by John Grafton (Dover Publications)

12 Gothic Tales, edited by Richard Dalby (Oxford University Press)

Classic Chillers, edited by E. M. Freeman (Globe Pequot Press)

12 Irish Ghost Stories, edited by Patricia Craig (Oxford University Press)

18 Best Stories by Edgar Allan Poe, edited by Chandler Brossard (Dell Publishing)

Short and Scary Thrillers, edited by Rebecca Rizzo (Globe Pequot Press)

The Hound of the Baskervilles, by Sir Arthur Conan Doyle

Frankenstein, by Mary Shelley

Scary Stories to Tell in the Dark, Alvin Schwartz and Stephen Gammel (HarperCollins)—for kids 9 and up

Headless Haunt and Other African-American Ghost Stories by James Haskin (HarperCollins)

Campfire Stories, Volumes I–III, edited by William W. Forgey, M.D. (Globe Pequot Press)

currant juice, and absinthe, and be ready to mix some creepy drinks, like a snakebite, made with equal parts cider and lager.

Once the party's begun, play atmospheric music, perhaps one of the following:

● *Edgar Allan Poe Suite* (by Baxter/Cacavas; Citadel)

● *Horror at the Movies* (Madacy Records)

● Spencer Lewis's compositions—including "A

Sense of Place," "Close to Home," and "Silence Between the Words"—create an image of village folk gathering during the harvest festival to dance a country jig (available from Quartz Recording, P.O. Box 20, Bethel, VT 05032 or www.quartzrecordings.com)

● *Elvira Presents Monster Hits* (Rhino)

● *Music for a Darkened Theatre* (by Danny Elfman; UNI/MCA)

● soundtrack from *Close Encounters of the Third Kind* (BMG/Arista)

● *Drew's Famous Monster Mash Party Music* (Turn Up the Music)

● *Scary Sound Effects* (WEA/Atlantic/Rhino)

● *Dr. Demento's Spooky Tunes and Scary Melodies* (WEA/Atlantic/Rhino)

● *Night on Bald Mountain* (by Mussorgsky; Telarc)

● Make your own tape combining *Phantom of the Opera* and *Sweeney Todd* music

Or listen to readings:

● Edgar Allan Poe's *The Pit and the Pendulum* (Folkways, 800-410-9815)

Children will love gathering the materials for and making this humorous wreath to hang from a barn, front door, or tree. Weave leaf clusters into a vine wreath, then tuck sumac branches along the top for hair or top-hat effect. For the eyes and nose, use an ice pick to make holes through the sides of pumpkins and the base of a gourd. Spear a bamboo skewer through the pumpkins and gourd to create one piece. Attach floral wire to the skewer in two places and hang from the top of the wreath.

- Washington Irving's *The Legend of Sleepy Hollow* (Folkways, 800-410-9815)
- *The Tell-tale Heart and Other Stories by Edgar Allan Poe* (Dover Publications, 516-294-7000)

Gather round the fireplace when it's time for party games. Have a costume contest, with the scariest, most original, and most foolish entries taking home silly prizes. Bob for apples and play pass-the-orange—you can't use your hands and the orange is tucked under your chin; the last person not to drop the orange wins. Or start a ghost story–telling round by giving each guest a twig. To begin, one person comes up with the opening sentence of a creepy story. A guest then throws a twig into the fire and continues the story until the twig is gone. Then the next guest throws his twig into the fire, taking up the thread of the tale.

Play an Irish game of prognostication: To discover "Who is my true love?," each person peels a long circular piece from an apple. The piece is thrown over the left shoulder, landing in the shape of the first letter of the true love's name. Or put pairs of nuts, named after couples, into the fire. If the nuts burn to ashes side by side, it means a long and happy life for the couple. A lot of crackling or parting of the nuts means discord will tarnish the relationship. For future prosperity, a nut that blazes brightly is preferable to one that smolders or pops.

A grouping of miniature pumpkins carved out to hold votive candles creates all the atmosphere needed on Halloween—or any autumn night, for that matter. Try this with other gourds of similar size. Choose pumpkins or gourds that are firm to the touch and that have shapely stems, then carve out a top from each pumpkin, large enough to accommodate a small votive candle, about 1 1/2 inches in diameter, and scoop out a hole about 2 inches deep.

block-print invitations

Invite your friends to a Halloween party with these bold cards that set the tone for the event, or send them as greeting cards. The pumpkin invitation at left in the photo is created by a block-printing process, a technique that makes it easy to create a large quantity of cards. Instructions for the other two invites are on the following pages.

x

1. For each invitation, cut a rectangle of orange paper about 10 by 3 inches. Trim one short edge with the scallop scissors. Fold in half crosswise, so that the scallop edge is a bit longer than the other.

2. Trim the printing block so that it is slightly smaller than the folded piece of paper. With a pencil, lightly draw your design onto the block. This is a reverse process: The lines you draw will be the non-inked part of the invitation. Using the linoleum cutter tool and blade, cut out the design (children should do this with the help of an adult.)

3. Squeeze a quarter-size blob of ink onto the glass. Roll the brayer back and forth to spread the ink (it may be sticky at first). Once the brayer is covered with an even coat of ink, roll it across the printing block.

4. Center and carefully place the front side of the invitation onto the inked block. Without shifting it, rub the paper hard, then peel away. Repeat with the remaining invitations, reinking the block each time.

MATERIALS

orange construction paper

black water-soluble block printing ink, such as Speedball

TOOLS

scallop-edged scissors

rubber printing block, such as Speedy Cut from Speedball

linoleum cutter tool and blade (available at art supply stores)

windowpane-size piece of glass or acrylic

brayer (ink roller available at art supply stores)

x

x

x

"boo" cutout invitations

Try a simple rhyming verse written on the inside of the invitation to tell the tale of your party's time, date, place, and costume theme. These invitations can also be made with blank store-bought cards, embellished with the cutouts.

1. For each invitation, cut a rectangle of white paper about 4 by 5 inches. Fold in half crosswise. Trim the short edges with the zigzag scissors.

2. Cut a rectangle of black paper about 4 by 2 ½-inches. With the white pencil, write your message (in this case the word BOO) lightly on the center of the paper and cut out with the X-Acto knife (don't worry about the insides of the letters yet). Discard the letters and apply glue stick to surrounding black. Center on the white folded card.

3. With the hole punch, punch out 4 black dots for the insides of the letters. Glue stick the dots in place, using tweezers to help handle the pieces.

❖　❖　❖

MATERIALS

white construction paper

black construction paper

TOOLS

zigzag- or scallop-edged scissors

white pencil

X-Acto knife

glue stick

hole punch

pumpkin cutout
invitations

This card is another example of the many different designs that can be created with boldly colored paper and a pair of scissors. Vary your design according to the kind of party you are having—depending on the paper and design you choose, this can be made to the height of sophistication or to please any child. Bats, witches, cats—any graphic shape will work, and you can adapt the size of the card to fit your design.

1. For each invitation, cut a rectangle of orange paper about 12 by 5 inches. Fold in half crosswise. Trim the 2 long edges with the zigzag scissors.

2. Cut a rectangle of black paper about 6 by 4½-inches. Cut out a moon on the upper right portion of the card with the X-Acto knife. Apply glue from the glue stick to the underside of the black paper and center on the folded orange paper. Trim any excess overhang with the X-Acto knife and ruler.

3. Cut out three 2-inch circles from the orange paper for the pumpkins. Apply glue from the glue stick and place on the invitation. From the black paper cut out facial features and glue stick them in place on the pumpkins, using tweezers to help handle the tiny pieces.

4. Cut 3 short lengths of green twine. Glue to the top of the pumpkins with craft glue.

❖   ❖   ❖

MATERIALS

orange construction paper

black construction paper

green twine

TOOLS

zigzag-edged scissors

X-Acto knife

glue stick

metal-edged ruler

craft glue

painted tablecloth

Bring out this tablecloth every year to set a festive mood at Halloween time. Painting images on black fabric would make for a moodier and scarier backdrop to a buffet feast. You could also make matching cotton napkins, repeating an icon from the tablecloth in a corner of each napkin.

1. Turn the sheeting under ¼ inch on all 4 sides. Press and glue down with the fabric glue.

2. With the colored pencils, lightly mark pumpkin, moon, and star designs on the cloth. For each color, mix together equal parts textile medium and paint. Paint the shapes and outline loosely with black.

3. Cut the rickrack into 4½-inch strips. Alternating colors, glue one end of each strip to the turned-in edges of the cloth. Let dry.

4. With machine stitching, top stitch along the edge of the cloth, securing the rickrack.

❖   ❖   ❖

MATERIALS

42-inch square white cotton sheeting

textile medium

orange, yellow, and black acrylic paint

20 packages orange, black, and white jumbo rickrack

TOOLS

fabric glue, such as Fabri-Tac

orange and yellow colored pencils

brushes

candy corn
place holders

Give your guests something to take home besides the shivers! For a sit-down dinner, place one of these at each table setting, or, at a more informal gathering, have a tray (lined with fall leaves, sphagnum moss, or black felt) of these goodie-filled painted pots waiting by the door for your friends to take with them as they leave the party.

1. With a sponge brush, paint the inside and outside of each pot with one coat of white paint. Let dry.

2. Paint a 1/2-inch stripe of yellow paint around the bottom edge of each pot. Let dry. Paint a 1 1/2-inch orange stripe above the yellow stripe of each pot, going a little bit up into the rim. Let dry. Paint another coat of white paint around the top 1/2 inch of the rim of each pot. Let dry.

3. With the zigzag scissors, cut tags out of the orange paper. Punch a hole in the upper left corner and write a name on each.

4. Cut 10- by 10-inch squares of cellophane. Place some candy in the center of each and gather the sides up around the candy. Twist a pipe cleaner around each to gather. Thread one end of each pipe cleaner through a tag and then coil the ends by wrapping around a pencil. Place the candy bags inside the pots.

❖   ❖   ❖

MATERIALS

2 1/2-inch-tall terra-cotta flower pots

white, yellow, and orange acrylic paint

orange construction paper

cellophane wrap

candy corn and other Halloween candy

orange pipe cleaners

TOOLS

sponge brushes

zigzag-edged scissors

hole punch

hanging carved
lanterns

Mischievous goblins need some light when moonglow isn't enough. These tin-can lanterns, once made, will last from year to year. Simple slits and circles will suffice to create scary grimaces or even black cats about to jump from the shadows. (The sharp edges of the cutouts do mean that this is not a children's project and that you should wear heavy work gloves.) Candles placed in each lantern cast a special glow that reflects off the sides of the can interiors. Hang them at various heights from trees or an arbor, or place them along a stone wall.

1. Clean the cans thoroughly and remove the tops.

2. Using the sawhorse or piece of wood to hold a can steady, hammer a nail through the can to make a starting hole. Wearing protective gloves, insert the tip of the knife blade into the hole and make an incision.

3. Cut out features with the knife. Keep in mind that simple lines are the most effective. It's best to imagine stylized primitive masks, where just a slash indicates a nose, mouth, eye, or whisker. For a nose, pull the knife straight down, then sideways; turn the knife back and forth so the bottom of the hole widens. Use the ice pick to make freckles and the pointed end of the bottle opener, pressed against the bottom of the can, to make teeth.

4. Punch 2 nail holes on opposite sides of the can and thread a piece of wire through them to make a long handle.

5. Repeat with additional cans to make more lanterns.

6. With the glue gun, glue a candle to the inside bottom of each can.

❖　　❖　　❖

MATERIALS

tin cans in assorted sizes and
   shapes (olive oil cans, tomato
   cans, soup cans)

wire for hanging cans

5-inch-tall candles

TOOLS

sawhorse or piece of wood

hammer and large nails

protective work gloves

heavy-duty knife

ice pick

bottle opener

hot glue gun and sticks

skeleton luminarias

In the Southwest, luminarias—paper bags filled with sand anchoring a candle—placed along a walkway are meant to guide the traveler. On Halloween, the familiar brown paper bags take on a slightly sinister quality as they lead small gremlins or dinner guests to Mr. Pumpkinhead, the jack-o'-lantern waiting by the door. The skeleton forms on the bags are printed by an easy process. If younger children are helping, simpler images such as a bat or cat can be tried. When you set the bags out, be sure they are completely open to prevent them from burning. Also position them along the walkway where they will not be knocked over by children in long costumes, tails, etc.

1. Cut the Styrofoam trays to 4- by 8-inch rectangles so they lie flat. With the cuticle stick, draw designs into the Styrofoam. This is a reverse process: A design you create will be the non-inked part of the bag.

2. Squeeze about 1 1/2 inches of ink onto the glass. Roll the brayer back and forth to spread the ink (it may be sticky at first). Once the brayer is covered with an even coat of ink, roll it across a Styrofoam image.

3. Press the the side of a brown paper bag onto the Styrofoam. Rub the paper bag with a large serving spoon, pressing the paper into the Styrofoam with a back and forth movement.

4. Carefully remove the bag and set it aside to dry (approximately 10 minutes). Reink the Styrofoam or use another piece with a different image and repeat the process with additional bags.

5. Open the bags and fill each 1 inch deep with sand. Light the candles in their glasses and ease them into the center of the sand in the bags.

❖ ❖ ❖

MATERIALS

black water-soluble block printing ink, such as Speedball

12 1/2- by 6-inch brown paper bags

sand

3-inch-tall votive candles in glass containers

TOOLS

Styrofoam trays (used for packing foods—ask your butcher for clean, unused trays or thoroughly wash used ones)

cuticle stick or any hard-tipped instrument, such as tip of paint brush handle, end of spoon, or dull pencil (to trace patterns in the Styrofoam)

windowpane-size piece of glass or acrylic

6- to 8-inch-wide brayer (ink roller available in art supply stores)

front door scarecrow

This funny fellow will greet visitors from Halloween through Thanksgiving. Children will love collecting the elements that make up his attire, from the old clothes to colorful fall leaves.

1. For the arms, with the $\frac{1}{8}$-inch drill bit, drill a hole, front to back, through the pole of the rake, 6 inches down from the neck. Drill another $\frac{1}{8}$-inch hole through the middle of the 24-inch branch. Place the branch over the pole, matching the holes. Insert the bolt and tighten with the nut. You can now rotate the arms into a perpendicular position.

2. For the eyes, cut two $\frac{3}{4}$-inch slices from the remaining branch with the saw. Hammer a nail into the center of each slice to create the pupil of the eye (you may want to drill a hole first to prevent any splitting). The nail should stick out beyond the wood in back. This will be used to wedge the eyes in place between the bamboo prongs.

3. For the nose, hold the gourd firmly and take off any stem that remains (or use the saw or sharp knife to cut it off). Screw the drywall screw partially into where you have removed the stem, leaving $\frac{1}{2}$ inch of the screw exposed. The head of the screw can then be slid into place and wedged between the prongs of the rake, as with the eyes. (It may help to use a wide-head screwdriver to separate the prongs of the rake.)

4. For the mouth, cut 2 lengths of twine and twist together. Slip them into position in between prongs of the rake.

5. Weave leaves and bittersweet or other vines in between prongs of the rake for hair. Dress the scarecrow with shirt, overalls, gloves, and bandana. Tie two 4-foot pieces of twine onto the arm branch at the "shoulders." Dangle the twine down each pant leg and tie on boots.

MATERIALS

large bamboo rake with wooden pole

24-inch branch, approximately the same diameter as the rake pole

$\frac{1}{2}$- by $\frac{1}{8}$-inch bolt with nut

branch, approximately 1 $\frac{1}{2}$-inch diameter

small gourd

1-inch drywall screw

green twine

leaves

bittersweet

old shirt, overalls, gloves, bandana, and boots

TOOLS

drill with $\frac{1}{8}$-inch drill bit

saw

hammer and 1 $\frac{1}{2}$-inch nails

❖ ❖ ❖

tissue paper ghosts

Ghosts have been a part of Halloween since it began. In ancient times, people believed that the souls or spirits of departed ones came back at this time of year to visit the living—and not always with the best intentions! Ghosts are also thought to appear to whisper of something the future holds. These lively little ghosts dance in a window, foretelling the fun and treats that are about to happen!

1. To make patterns, draw simple ghosts on the oak tag and cut out.

2. Place the patterns on a piece of tissue paper and trace around. With the craft scissors, carefully cut out the ghosts.

3. With the medium hole punch, make eyes. With the small hole punch, make one hole at the top of each head. Pull 12-inch pieces of thread through the small hole and knot.

4. Attach the hole reinforcers to the ends of the threads and hang the ghosts on the window mullion. Trim excess thread.

❖   ❖   ❖

MATERIALS

white tissue paper

white thread

white hole reinforcers (from office supply stores)

TOOLS

oak tag

small craft scissors

medium hole punch

small hole punch

spooky tip

To make your windows even scarier, paint spooky swirls on the glass. Line the window sash with masking tape before you begin. Mix 1/2 tablespoon of white powdered tempera with 1 tablespoon clear dishwashing soap to a creamy consistency in a foil muffin tin (or use a product called Glass Wax, available in hardware stores). Apply to the window glass in ghostly swirls with a slightly damp sponge or paper towel. To remove the dried paint, simply rub off with a dry paper towel.

spooky cutout garlands

No self-respecting haunted house would be caught "dead" without bats, black cats, jack-o'-lanterns, and at least a few ghosts to create a scary atmosphere. Fun and easy-to-make, these festive garlands can be hung just about everywhere—in doorways, across the mantel, or along the edge of a table. Store them carefully and you will be able to use them for many Halloweens to come.

1. With a photocopier, enlarge the templates below 200 percent (or design patterns of your own). With the templates, make patterns from the construction paper.

2. Cut a 36-inch strip from the orange lightweight paper. Fold, accordion style, with each panel the same width as the pumpkin pattern. Trace the pumpkin on the first panel, making sure the pattern touches both right and left folded edges.

3. Cut through all the folded strip layers, being sure that you don't cut off all of the folded edges. Cut eyes and mouth. Unfold. With the needle and thread, thread a piece of string to each end of the cutout.

4. Repeat with bat, cat, and ghost designs on different colored paper.

MATERIALS

orange, white, and black light-weight paper, 36 inches wide

TOOLS

construction paper

needle and thread

❖   ❖   ❖

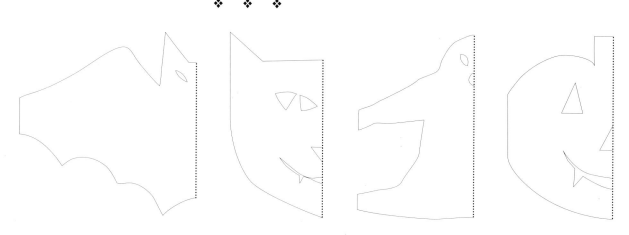

halloween
lampshade

Combining black, the symbol of the "darker" side of Halloween, and deep yellow or orange, the colors of the harvest, turns a simple decorating project into a tribute to an age-old celebration. Adapt this lampshade by gluing silhouetted cutouts of a black cat or witch on a broom to a non-opaque lampshade—it will add ambiance to any room!

1. Glue the pom-pom fringe to the outside bottom edge of the lampshade a little at a time, using clothespins to hold the fringe in place while the glue dries.

2. Glue the rickrack on the top edge of the fringe, again holding with clothespins until dried.

3. Evenly space orange dots around the main part of shade.

❖ ❖ ❖

MATERIALS

black pom-pom ball fringe (long enough to fit around bottom of lampshade)

black lampshade

orange medium rickrack

orange ¾-inch-round dot labels

TOOLS

craft glue

clothespins

day of the dead

The American Halloween has its roots in Celtic beliefs, one of which was that the dead return for a day. Other cultures have similar observances. In Mexico, the Day of the Dead is celebrated on November 1. The night before—October 31—families visit cemeteries, lighting candles to help the souls of their dead relatives return to the land of the living for just one night. They welcome the dead back with food, candles, and decorated skulls made from sugar and water.

checkerboard frame

Don't let a costumed child in the thrall of Halloween excitement escape the camera. Every year, take a photograph of your own children before they leave to go trick-or-treating as well as those who come to the door—the pictures will be treasured. And what better way to proudly display this year's costumes than in this lightly distressed wooden frame?

1. Remove the backing materials and glass from the frame. With a rag, rub the frame with the white paint. With a clean part of the rag, rub off most of the paint. Let dry. In the same way, rub in the yellow paint and rub off. Let dry.

2. With the orange pencil, lightly sketch a checkerboard design on the frame. Paint in orange squares. Let dry. For a distressed look, lightly sand in some places and leave others as is. With the brush, paint the inner rim of the frame black. Assemble the frame with your picture, glass, and backing materials.

MATERIALS

unpainted wooden picture frame

white, yellow, orange, and black acrylic paint

TOOLS

rags

orange colored pencil

sandpaper

small brush

spook-out felt pillows

It doesn't take witchcraft to make these, just simple sewing skills. Felt is easy to work with (it won't slip and slide while being cut and sewn), and the result looks like American folk art.

1. Transfer or trace cat, moon, and star designs onto the backing of the fusible web. Iron to a piece of black felt and cut out the shapes. From the orange felt, cut out one $15\frac{1}{2}$-inch square for the front and two $15\frac{1}{2}$- by 9-inch rectangles for the back.

2. To make the pillow borders, iron a 15- by 3-inch piece of fusible web to a 15- by 3-inch piece of black felt. Remove the backing and iron to another piece of felt (you are putting the adhesive between 2 layers of felt to strengthen the fabric). On a 15- by 3-inch strip of contact paper, draw a border design that has 7 connecting triangles, each about $2\frac{1}{2}$ inches across the base. Cut out with the X-Acto knife and ruler. Attach the contact paper borders to the felt and cut along the edges of the paper. Peel off the contact paper. Press down any fuzz pick-up with a hot iron. Repeat to make 3 more borders.

3. Place the felt borders along each side of the $15\frac{1}{2}$-inch orange square, the points facing inward. Baste in position.

4. On one long edge of a backing piece, turn in the fabric 1 inch and press. Center and pin a 10-inch Velcro strip along this turned-in edge and sew 2 parallel lines along its length, securing the Velcro in place. On the second piece of backing, pin the matching Velcro in the same place as on the first and sew in place. Remove the pins.

5. Place the Velcro strips on top of each other to make one closed back. Pin the 2 back pieces to the front square, right sides together and the border pieces on the inside. Trim the back pieces, if necessary, to be

MATERIALS

two 15-inch pillow forms or two 1-pound bags of polyester fiberfill

1 yard paper-backed fusible web, such as HeatnBond Ultra Hold

2 yards black felt

2 yards orange felt

20 inches Velcro sew-on tape

TOOLS

3/4 yard contact paper

X-Acto knife

metal-edged ruler

the same size as the front. With a $\frac{1}{4}$-inch seam allowance, sew front to back. Remove the pins and trim the seams. Turn right side out.

6. Insert a magazine or flat newspaper inside the pillow cover. Remove the backing from the black shapes and iron to the pillow front. Add fabric glue to some pieces if they don't stay pressed down. Stuff the pillow with a pillow form or fiberfill. Glue the open back edges on the sides of the Velcro closed.

7. Repeat with a pumpkin design to make a black pillow with an orange cutout.

❖   ❖   ❖

gourd candles

Fill a room with candlelight and it sets the stage for a moody evening. Candles can be made at home quite easily, and using small winter squash as molds creates graceful shapes. Choose different color tablets to represent the range of harvest tones.

1. Cut the tops off the squash and hollow out the insides. (For hubbard squash, scrape out the seeds with a large spoon. For acorn squash, use the melon baller to scoop out the flesh, following the natural grooves of the squash, making the grooves as deep as possible, and smoothing them with the back of a spoon.)

2. Melt the wax in the top part of the double boiler over—not in—boiling water. As the wax melts, add color tablets. If you want to make different colored candles, melt the wax in batches, adding different color tablets each time.

3. Meanwhile, cut lengths of wick a few inches longer than the squash are tall. Attach the wick tabs to the wicks.

4. When the wax is completely melted, carefully pour into a squash. Drop in one wick tab, with the wick attached, and let it settle to the bottom. Lay a pencil across the top of the squash and drape the end of the wick over it so it is as centered as possible. Repeat, in batches if you like, to make more candles. Let the candles harden completely, 5 to 6 hours, then peel the outside of the squash away from the wax.

❖ ❖ ❖

MATERIALS

acorn and hubbard squash (and others, if available)

bee's wax or regular paraffin candle wax (allow about $\frac{1}{2}$ pound for each candle)

yellow, orange, coral, and/or purple wax color tablets

candle wicks

wick tabs

TOOLS

melon baller

double boiler

halloween
photo album

Make a Halloween album and give your photographs and children's drawings a final resting place!

1. To make the covers: Cut out four 9- by 12-inch pieces of black felt. Write your title on the embroidery paper in stylized letters. Baste the paper to one piece of felt. Embroider with the thread. Remove the paper. Draw a hat, jack-o'-lantern, and broom on the backing of the fusible web and iron to the orange felt. Cut out, remove the backing, and iron to the same piece of black felt.

2. Baste the lettered piece of felt to a second piece and blanket stitch together. Repeat with the 2 remaining pieces of felt for the back.

3. Cut two 11- by 14-inch pieces of fusible web. Iron one to the wrong side of a piece of lining fabric. Remove the backing and carefully position the cardboard on the fabric. Press with an iron. Fold the edges over the back of the cardboard and iron. Repeat with the remaining piece of fabric.

4. On the nonfabric side of one piece of cardboard, with the bone-scorer, score 1 inch from the edge on a long side (to allow the front cover to fold). Position and glue the front cover to the uncovered side of the scored cardboard. Repeat with the back cover and the other piece of cardboard.

5. One-half inch in from the edge and 2¾ inches from the top and bottom, make 2 small slits with the X-Acto knife into each cover. Use the awl to push through and make holes. Set in the eyelets.

6. Stack the pages and place between the covers. Mark the paper through the eyelets. Punch holes in the paper. Assemble the book. Thread the ribbon and rickrack through the holes and tie in front.

MATERIALS

1 yard black felt

2 skeins white embroidery thread and needle

¾ yard paper-backed fusible web, such as HeatnBond Ultra Hold

scrap orange felt

two 11- by 14-inch pieces orange and black check fabric for lining

two 8½- by 11¾-inch pieces cardboard

4 eyelets

twelve 8½- by 11-inch pieces black construction paper for pages

50 inches black and white check ribbon

50 inches baby-size orange rickrack

TOOLS

6- by 6-inch piece embroidery paper, such as Stitch and Tear

bone-scoring tool

X-Acto knife

awl

fabric glue, such as Fabri-Tac

hole punch

❖　❖　❖

chapter two

the jack-o'-lantern

Place even a single uncarved pumpkin in a window or on a porch, and you have taken the first step to creating the **atmosphere** of Halloween. Making a jack-o'-lantern is a must, however. No special skills are necessary, just the willingness to let your imagination be your guide.

The **local farmers'** market or pumpkin patch is the place to start—there everyone can choose the pumpkin that strikes his fancy. Pumpkin-picking can make for an afternoon of great fun. Be choosy—don't pick a **pumpkin** that is too huge, or it could take hours to carve. Keep in mind that taller, rounder pumpkins are easiest to **carve**, and lopsided ones naturally look scarier once they have a face. Check the bottom of the pumpkin to make sure it is flat, otherwise it might fall over or roll away. It's best to avoid **bruised** pumpkins, or ones that are quite soft, since they won't last as long.

A face is not the only design to carve. A simple first initial would delight any child, especially when it is illuminated by a candle. For the final touch, rub cinnamon inside the pumpkin top. When the candle is lit and the lid replaced—partway, so it doesn't burn—a cinnamon fragrance will fill the air.

Miniature pumpkins too small for a carved face make perfect holders for votive candles. This carving project takes no time at all and the results are dramatic—tiny lanterns placed on a staircase or down the center of a table make a memorable decoration.

The Story of the Jack-o'-Lantern

There are probably as many tales in Irish folklore about the origins of the jack-o'-lantern as there are ways to carve a pumpkin. In fact, the original jack-o'-lantern was not a pumpkin at all, but a humble turnip or, in some stories, a gnarly, beetlike vegetable called a mangel-wurzel. But once the Irish encountered the large native American pumpkin, the small, hard turnip was history. With its bright orange shell and round shape, the pumpkin made a much more formidable jack-o'-lantern than a turnip.

Along with the great Irish migration to America in the 1850's came the legend of the jack-o'-lantern. The story begins with Jack, a nasty, hard-drinking miser. One tale finds Jack walking down a country road when the Devil comes to claim him. Wily in his ways, Jack asks for one last apple from a nearby tree, and cajoles the Devil into climbing up to pluck the apple for him. As soon as the Devil is off the ground, Jack quickly carves a cross in the trunk, trapping the Devil in the branches above.

This is not the only time that Jack outwits the Devil. Another legend has Jack asking the Devil for a coin for a last drink. He then talks the Devil into changing into that coin, puts the coin into his wallet, draws a cross on the wallet, and imprisons the Devil there. In exchange for his freedom, the Devil promises not to take Jack's soul for another ten years. "Promise me you will *never* take my soul," retorts Jack, "and I'll let you go." The Devil agrees, and back to hell he goes. Years later, worn out and tired, Jack is ready for eternal rest. But he is turned away from heaven for his mean ways on earth; and when he tries the gates of hell, the Devil refuses to take him in. So that Jack does not have to roam the earth in darkness, the Devil tosses him a lighted coal from the fires of hell. Jack pops the coal into the turnip he is gnawing on, and carries it as a lantern as he searches for a final resting place.

Tools & Supplies

Ask a panel of experienced pumpkin carvers about their favorite tools and each person will tell you something different. Long, slender kitchen knives are preferred by some because they cut a clean, smooth line; others vouch for a stubby knife with a serrated edge (easier to control, they say). Around Halloween time, stores with holiday supplies carry pumpkin-carving kits that contain tools designed for children to use easily and safely. Art supply stores carry sculpting tools that make it easy to carve with great detail.

Store your pumpkins in a cool, dark place and do not carve until a day or two before Halloween; once carved, most pumpkins only last a few days. When you're ready to carve, gather the tools you need:

• Lots of newspaper is necessary to protect your work space.

• A melon scooper and serving-size spoons are great for scooping out and scraping the insides of pumpkins.

• A pencil makes it easy to sketch designs on the pumpkin.

• An eight-inch carving knife with a narrow blade will do the carving.

• A small paring knife with a narrow blade works best for corners and curves, and also is good for neatening rough edges. Use the handle end to tap out circles and other shapes.

• Different sizes of candles are needed to rest inside the pumpkin; the 3-inch-high ones found in supermarkets are usually the right size.

• Small saucers or votive glasses are used to hold candles in place. Drip a few drops of hot wax on a small saucer that will fit easily through the opening in the pumpkin, or use

Use an 8-inch carving knife and large serving spoon to cut and scoop out these little pumpkins. Cut 6 or more 1/2-inch-wide slits from the top to bottom of each one. Helping to clean out the flesh and seeds and lining up the pumpkins according to size are jobs for little hands. Drawing the crescents and carving their shapes is best left to the adults, while the children stay busy separating the seeds for roasting (see page 96 for recipe).

one lit candle to melt the bottom of another candle. Hold the candle in place on the plate while the wax hardens.

Optional Tools—for Adult Use Only

If you want to go beyond the simple triangles and squares of everyday jack-o'-lanterns, some additional tools are required:

● A round hole cutter, available in art supply stores, made of stainless steel is good for cutting perfect circles in jack-o'-lanterns. An apple corer works well, too.

● A loop, a clay tool available in art supply stores, is perfect for making spirals and other designs that don't go all the way through the pumpkin skin, creating a translucent effect.

● Medium wood gouges—sculpture carving tools available in art supply stores—can be used for layering and for circles. Place the tip of the gouge under the jack-o'-lantern's eyes and tap downward on the handle with a wooden mallet. This will cut away the top layer of pumpkin flesh to create a little teardrop for a "sad" look. Or insert the gouge into the pumpkin flesh, turn, and pull out to complete a circular shape.

● A power drill with a hole cutter drill bit makes carving larger pumpkins with thick shells easier. Use them to control the cutting of exact designs, such as the lightning and stars on the white pumpkins on page 52.

Tips for Pumpkin Carving

● Choose a large, plump pumpkin with a long, strong stem for the best jack-o'-lantern.

● Sketch out your ideas on paper before you draw and carve the pumpkin. Perhaps the natural shape of the pumpkin will inspire a design.

● Keep a decent distance between the eyes, nose, and mouth when carving, or else the pumpkin might collapse.

● Select candles that are the right height for the size of the pumpkins. Candles that are too tall will burn the top of the pumpkin.

● Save the pumpkin seeds for a crunchy, nutritious snack (see page 96).

Pumpkin Carving with Children

● Never let children carve pumpkins alone.

● Let children do as much of the work as possible, with the exception of using sharp tools.

● Make the features large so that they are easy to cut out. This also means more light will shine from the pumpkin.

● A child too young to use a knife can help draw the face and scoop out the seeds.

Pumpkin Growing

A pumpkin is a member of the gourd family, from the genus *Cucurbita*, which includes all varieties of pumpkins, gourds, and winter and summer squash. The Pepos varieties of the Northeast—including 'Big Autumn,' 'Autumn

Gold,' 'Happy Jack,' 'Harvest Moon,' and 'Jumpin Jack'—are the big, traditional orange pumpkins most familiar as carving pumpkins.

Pumpkins are easy to grow, as long as you choose a variety that is right for your climate and garden. With growth periods as short as 90 days and as long as 130 days, there is a variety of pumpkin that can be grown successfully in all zones. For example, the 'Cheese' pumpkin and the 'Golden Cushaw' both grow well in hot, humid climates. In southern gardens, 'Sugar' and 'Winter Luxury' pumpkins do well. The cold, wet weather of the north is good for 'Lumina,' a pearly white pumpkin, and for 'Small Sugar.'

Pumpkins need plenty of room to grow, and adequate planting space also discourages diseases. After planting, feed every three weeks with compost, 5-10-5 fertilizer, or fish emulsion, and make sure to water well. Unless your pumpkins are growing in well-drained, sandy soil, place a wooden shingle under each one in the late summer to protect against rot caused by contact with wet soil.

Don't be in too much of a hurry to harvest: Pumpkins can bask in the autumn sun until the vines yellow and die, since only a hard freeze will harm them. Though they take up a lot of space, pumpkins are a wonderful sight, especially late in the season when their rich hues add a final burst of color to the garden.

If a champion pumpkin is what you are after, the best variety to grow is 'Atlantic Giant,' bred just for its huge size. Should tasty pumpkin flesh be the goal, smaller pumpkins such as 'Small Sugar' and 'Sugar' can be turned into pumpkin pies, and their size also makes them good for jack-o'-lanterns. The seeds of a pumpkin are edible—roasted, salted, and eaten by the handful, they make a tasty snack. For the best seeds, grow 'Trick or Treat' pumpkins.

Children really enjoy tending pumpkins and marking their progress in the garden. They especially delight in the smaller varieties grown for decorative purposes, such as the three-inch-wide miniatures 'Sweetie Pie' and 'Jack Be Little.' Like all other pumpkins, these miniatures are edible, and when prepared like acorn squash (halved and baked with butter, a touch of nutmeg, and cinnamon), children find them delicious to eat.

Ghost-like in appearance, novelty white pumpkins are growing in popularity. Among the favorites are 'Lumina' and 'Valenciano.' When children are too young to handle carving tools, the smooth surface of a white pumpkin such as the mini 'Baby Boo' makes a good place for them to draw or paint a Halloween face.

jack o' lanterns

In Celtic times, huge bonfires were set to frighten away the evil spirits believed to wander the land on All Hallow's Eve. Much later, Irish villagers paraded from house to house on this night, carrying lanterns made from turnips and beets. Once they immigrated here, the Irish found that the native American pumpkin was easier to carve and made a much bigger lantern. So the jack-o'-lantern was born.

1. Cover the work surface with newspapers. Cut off the tops of the pumpkins with the carving knife by making a 6-inch circular cut around the stems. Remove the tops and hollow out the pumpkins with a large spoon.

2. Sketch features on the pumpkin surfaces with a pencil. Cut out features with the carving knife and paring knife. To make a circle, insert the gouge into the pumpkin by tapping the gouge's handle with a hammer and twisting. Punch out the piece. For a 3-D effect, cut narrow, triangular holes in the nose areas and insert carrot pieces.

3. Without cutting through the pumpkins, use the loop to create wrinkles, hair, and other surface details by inserting the top of the loop and pulling just enough that the top orange layer of skin comes off.

4. Melt the bottom of the candle and anchor it to the glass container. Insert the candles in the pumpkins and light with fireplace matches. Leave the tops off the pumpkins to prevent the candles from extinguishing.

MATERIALS

large pumpkins in a variety of heights and shapes

carrot pieces for noses

votive candles in medium-size glass containers

TOOLS

8-inch carving knife

small paring knife

medium wood gouge

loop tool (available in art supply stores)

fireplace matches

pumpkins with personality

By setting it on its side, a pumpkin can go from round and plump to just plain comical. Around Halloween, there are so many pumpkins to choose from at farm stands and garden stores that finding a few with humorous potential should be easy and fun. Look for tall, skinny, or odd-shaped pumpkins with long, thick stems. The actual "carving" takes only a few minutes, as it is not necessary to clean out the insides. And since they are not hollowed out, they will stay fresher longer, and can later be used for baking.

1. Cover the work surface with newspapers.

2. Turn each pumpkin to a side on which it will rest solidly. With the carving tools, create eyes, mouths, and teeth (see page 56). Use the loop to create surface details, like teeth and whites of eyes. For circles, use a half-round carving tool or drill and drill bit. For slits, use the carving knife. Insert cranberries, nuts, or grapes in narrow slits to create eyes.

MATERIALS

large pumpkins with stems intact (choose unusual shapes)

cranberries, nuts, and/or grapes

TOOLS

carving tools, such as a half-round carving tool and medium wood gouge (available in art supply stores)

drill and 1-inch hole cutter drill bit

8-inch carving knife

chapter three

trick or treat

Trick-or-treating is just as enduring an American folk tradition as pumpkin carving. Originating in **ancient customs** designed to scare the spirits of the underworld, these rituals are today simply part of an evening of **fun**. Though we no longer fear the supernatural, asking for treats by going from house to house in **disguise** on a dark, cold night is one way we honor our past. Whether you live in a rural area or in a city, there are many tricks to making October 31 memorable. In my neighborhood, the festivities begin at sundown, with a parade of children in **colorful** costumes that starts in a local park and eventually spills out onto the street. Parents receive a list of homes participating in trick or treating—and then the fun begins. A **jack-o'-lantern** marks each door as children and their parents, also in costume, parade from door to door, to be greeted by a witch or goblin holding out a basket of goodies.

We have the Victorians to thank for bringing back today's popular custom of dressing up in **costumes** and **masks**. They brought their genteel sensibilities to Halloween, diluting the ancient, darker practices of the night by inviting guests into their homes for a party. The parties were themed, and every guest was required to wear a clever costume. Toward the end of the 19th century, trick-or-treating became popular in the United States, its origins in the Irish practice of asking for food for the poor—good luck came to those who gave, mischief and bad luck threatened those who refused.

The first piece of equipment every child needs when venturing out to trick-or-treat is a Halloween goodie bag. Decorating a bag is a project a child can do on his or her own, or at a party where the totes are taken home as

favors and used later on during the neighborhood rounds. Use the simple silhouette shapes that symbolize Halloween to turn a solid-color shopping bag into part of the costume. Cut the shapes out of black and orange construction paper and paste them on both sides of a good-sized paper shopping bag with sturdy handles. Each child can sign his or her name on the bottom corner for instant identification.

Planning and making a costume continues to be the best way to get into the spirit of the event, especially if the supplies for it are scavenged or inexpensive and inventive. Saving bits and pieces that will make up costumes and decorations can become a year-round project.

Dressed-up children are proud of their costumes, and one way to turn a helter-skelter run through the neighborhood into an enjoyable evening for everyone is to organize a Halloween parade, which adds pageantry to trick-or-treating. A neighborhood parade can include everyone who wants to participate—grown-ups too! Plan a route through a local park, or arrange to block off some side streets to traffic. Hot apple cider served at the last stop will warm even the coldest bones.

A visit to a haunted house along the trick-or-treat route will make Halloween night memorable (see pages 18 and 19 for some ideas on creating a haunted house).

safety tips

Accompany the kids to costume parades and block parties.

Check that your child will not trip on a costume that is too long or too big. Long hems can be sewn, or held in place with iron-on hem tape.

Reflective tape and glow-in-the-dark paints can be used on costumes and trick-or-treat bags to make adults and kids more visible at night.

Beware of lit candles in jack-o'-lanterns, burning leaves, and cigarettes, since most costume fabrics are not treated with flame retardants.

haunted happenings

California—San Jose: Take a flashlight tour of the Winchester Mystery House, 525 South Winchester Blvd; 408-247-2101.

Louisiana—New Orleans: Lafayette #1 Cemetery, Washington Ave., and St. Louis #1 Cemetery, Basin St. (which is the oldest cemetery in the city). Visit the tomb of Voodoo Priestess Marie Leveau. For tour information, call 800-672-6124.

Maryland—Baltimore: The city's oldest cemetery and the final resting place of Edgar Allan Poe is Westminster Hall Burying Ground at Fayette and Greene Streets. Tour the catacombs as well as the graveyard. Call 410-706-2072 for a schedule of special events held on Halloween.

Massachusetts—Salem: tours of haunted houses and the Salem Witch Museum; 978-744-1692.

New York—New Rochelle: New Rochelle's Famous Haunted House, 444 Quaker Ridge Rd.; 914-632-5700.

New York—Sleepy Hollow: Celebrate Legend Weekend, three days of special Halloween events and reenactments in Tarrytown and Sleepy Hollow. Visit Sunnyside, the home of Washington Irving, and listen to a reading of "The Legend of Sleepy Hollow;" 914-631-8200. Other related events are held at the Old Dutch Church, Route 9, Sleepy Hollow; 914-631-1123.

Tennessee—Chattanooga: Haunted Swamp, Chattanooga Nature Center; 423-821-1160.

Tennessee—Jonesborough: Ghost Story Concerts, part of the National Storytelling Festival; 800-525-4514, 423-753-2171.

Texas—Austin: Bat Spectacular, Congress Avenue Bridge. Each night at dusk from March until early November a colony of over one million bats emerges from its home under the bridge to forage for insects across the way; 516-327-9721.

Washington—Granite Falls: Visit the abandoned mining town of Monte Cristo, Route 92, Mountain Loop Highway; 425-348-5802.

Washington—Roche Harbor: Ghostly goings-on in Washington State's San Juan Islands at The Mausoleum, Hotel de Haro; 800-451-8910.

www.ghostweb.com—clearinghouse for ghost researchers, offers a list of Web sites and e-mail addresses for local clubs affiliated with the International Ghost Hunter's Society.

costume ideas

If you are short on time or not skilled with a needle and thread, try these non-sewing costume ideas.

forest sprite Gather large fall leaves and glue gun, staple, or pin them all over a green or brown turtleneck and leggings (these can be old clothes, dyed). Attach more leaves to a headband. With face paint, make green circles around the eyes, a white mouth, and a brown face.

pirate A striped pull-over, a red vest, dark pants tucked into boots, and a bandana tied around the head are the basics. Add an eye patch made from black paper and tied on with elastic. Don't forget a large gold hoop earring and cutlass, made of cardboard spray-painted silver, tied at the waist.

black cat The base clothes are a black turtleneck and tights. For a tail, stuff one leg from an old pair of black tights with rags and pin to the tights. Glue two small cardboard triangles to a headband, and add a black eye mask and face-paint whiskers to complete the ensemble.

fairy Start with a plain, long-sleeved, white dress that is long and full. Make a cardboard crown and glue on glitter. Make a wand by gluing a cardboard star to the end of a stick. Fairy wings can be created by covering two hangers with tinfoil, bending the tops of the hangers sideways and pinning them to the dress with large safety pins.

bum or tramp Raid Dad's closet for old, oversized clothes like a frayed shirt, worn-out jacket, shiny trousers, and a floppy hat. Add a long stick with a hobo sack tied on one end and lots of soot on the cheeks. A cigar completes the picture.

goblin Make a mask from a brown paper bag that goes over the head and rests on the shoulders. Mark large eyes, a nose, and a mouth carefully and cut out. Trim the mask with glued-on crepe paper or construction paper (for wild hair) and draw on some scary goblin details with markers. An old bathrobe or dark sweatsuit is the only other thing needed.

robot For the head, spray-paint a paper bag silver and cut out eye holes. Attach pipe cleaners with duct tape for antennae, and draw square eyes, a nose, and a mouth with a marker. Cut a hole (for the head) in the bottom of a large cardboard box; cut out holes for the arms. Spray-paint silver or cover the box with aluminum foil. Glue on buttons, small paper cups, and other found objects to create the controls, or draw shapes for controls with a marker.

fortune teller Start with a full, long skirt and oversized white blouse. Wrap a necktie around the waist and a scarf around the head, and add a big hoop earring and lots of necklaces. A shawl and brightly colored lipstick, a pack of playing cards, and a crystal ball (a Styrofoam ball covered in foil) are the accessories.

scarecrow Cut holes for eyes and a nose out of a brown paper bag and draw a big mouth in a smile. Glue straw (or lots of tall dry weeds from a field) or strips of brown paper on top for hair.

Put on a loose shirt and baggy pants and stuff straw or more strips into the sleeves and at the bottoms of the pants, extending over the hands and shoes. Tie a cord around the wrists and ankles to keep the straw in. Top with a floppy hat that has straw or strips of paper glued inside so they hang down and stick out like scarecrow hair.

ladybug or other critters Adapt this for other bugs, a turtle, or a bird. Cut two large pieces of oak tag or poster board in large circles and paint them red. Add small black dots. Cut an eyemask out of black construction paper, glue on pipe cleaners for feelers, and tie on with string. Create a sandwich board by stapling the two boards across the top, leaving an opening for the head. Wear black, green, or brown clothing appropriate to the critter.

other suggestions

Stimulate your creative imagination by scouring through mail-order catalogs, party store circulars, and costume shops for ideas.

Embellish any clothing—a solid-colored skirt, vest, leggings, sweatshirt, or cape—with bold cutout images sewn or painted on. Or cut fusible products, from the interfacing department at the local fabric store, into shapes and iron onto sweatshirts or other clothing. These products are also handy to give fabric weight (when you're making wings or a skirt).

If you have a few children, dress them in different animal costumes and have Dad dress as Noah shepherding his menagerie to the ark.

Make a poncho to be worn over sweats or a leotard by cutting any large, fairly heavyweight piece of fabric, such as felt, satin, or brocade, into a donut shape. Embellish with cutouts.

Vests are an easy way for an adult to dress up. Change fabrics and trim to fit the theme, from cowboy to cheerleader, gypsy to disco king.

Instant mask: Pop the lenses from a pair of old sunglasses and decorate the rims with feathers, glitter, and rhinestones.

Buy inexpensive bridal tulle to make a beautiful ballerina's skirt. A little girl can wear it over a leotard or shiny bathing suit. Gather layers of fabric with an elastic band, which doesn't require much sewing.

To keep warm on a cold Halloween night, pair a fleece sweatshirt with matching pants and add mouse ears or insect antennae on a headband.

Use neons, glitters, or brightly colored fabric paints to decorate clothing and create imaginative, eerie effects with a glow-in-the-dark look, which will also keep your child visible in the darkness.

Paint large brown paper bags with animal faces and cut 2 large holes for eyes. Use paint or markers to create whiskers, raccoon eyes, or a little dog nose.

tricksters' treats

Trick-or-treating has its origins in Irish traditions of long ago, but it has been enthusiastically embraced by modern children, who promise to spare the trick for the treat. These little bundles are a fun way to wrap up candy as a reward for trick-or-treaters, or to give away as party favors.

1. For about half the treats, cut 6-inch squares of double-layered cheesecloth. For the others, unfold an orange napkin. Unfold a black napkin and place it on top of the orange napkin at a 45-degree angle. Repeat with more napkins.

2. Pile handfuls of jelly beans in the center of each cheesecloth square and each set of napkins. Use the licorice string to tie each packet into a pouch and place a spider on each.

3. Place the bundles in a shallow bowl or tray. Set the platter on the spider webbing near the door. Pull the webbing around the platter at different angles, anchoring it to the table or a wall with thumbtacks.

❖ ❖ ❖

MATERIALS

1 package cheesecloth

1 package orange cocktail-size paper napkins

1 package black cocktail-size paper napkins

orange and black jelly beans

black string licorice

plastic spiders

fake spider webbing (available from stores with Halloween supplies)

TOOLS

thumbtacks

witch's candy bowl

See who will dare pluck a treat from this scary bowl! This make-together project for children and parents will thrill little trick-or-treaters. If a party is in the Halloween plans, put Ms. Witch to work as a centerpiece. (Don't forget to store her for next year's celebration.)

1. Make the papier-mâché paste: In a medium saucepan, bring 2 cups of the water to a boil. In a small bowl, combine the flour and remaining 2 cups water. Stir into the boiling water in the saucepan; return to a boil. Remove from the heat and stir in the sugar. Let cool and thicken, about 30 minutes.

2. For the hat, roll the piece of paper into a cone about 10 inches tall; tape to hold shut, then trim the bottom edge to make it even. Make a donut-shaped brim from the oak tag by cutting out a 9-inch circle, then cutting a 3 1/2-inch circle inside that. Tape the brim to the cone.

3. Blow the balloon up to approximately 10 inches by 8 inches; tie closed. Cut a 4 1/2-inch circle of cardboard and attach it to the large (bottom) end of the balloon with Scotch tape.

4. Dip newspaper strips into the papier-mâché paste and, one by one, apply to the outside of the hat and the underside of the brim, covering completely. Make 4 layers of papier mâché. Let dry.

5. Dip more strips into the paste and apply to the balloon and base, starting at the base and working up toward the neck of the balloon. Leave an uncovered area at the top about 5 inches wide. Apply 4 layers of papier mâché, adding facial features with pieces of crumpled paper. (We added eye brows, slight bumps for eyes, a large nose, chin, lips, and teeth.) Let dry 24 to 48 hours, until the surface is completely hard and dry and there are no soft spots.

MATERIALS

papier-mâché paste: 4 cups cold water, 1/2 cup flour, and 3 tablespoons sugar

10-inch balloon

cardboard

11- by 17-inch piece paper

11- by 17-inch piece oak tag

newspaper ripped into 1-inch-wide strips

white, black, green, and bright red acrylic paint

three 8 1/2- by 11-inch pieces black construction paper

TOOLS

paint brushes

craft glue

clothespins

6. Pop the balloon and remove. Paint the inside and outside of the witch's head and the hat with white paint. Let dry. Paint the inside and outside of the hat with 2 coats of black paint, letting the paint dry between coats. Paint the inside and outside of the witch's head with 2 coats of green paint, letting the paint dry between coats. Paint the face with red, white, and black paint.

7. For the witch's hair: Cut the construction paper lengthwise into 4 strips each. Fold each strip back and forth the short way, into a skinny accordion. Cut each strip into narrower strips to make strands of kinky hair, but don't cut all the way through to the end—leave a tab at the top. Glue hair to the rim of the bowl with craft glue, using clothespins to hold the hair in place while it dries.

devil costume

Who could be afraid of this imp of a devil? For an easier version, make just the tail and horns, then attach to red pants and a red headband. This makes about a size 4, but it can easily go larger, just by making the cape longer.

CAPE

1. Adjust the cape pattern so that the length will come a bit below the child's hip. Using the adjusted pattern, cut out a double layer of felt, aligning the fold with the fold mark on the pattern. Try the cape on the child and see if you need to make any adjustments to the neck hole. The cape should overlap at the front by 1½ inches. If you make any adjustments to the neck, remember to extend the collar horizontally by the same amount before cutting it out.

2. Using the collar pattern, cut out 2 pieces of felt. Pin and sew the collar together along the sides and top (longer) edge, using a ¼-inch seam allowance. Turn right side out and top stitch ¼ inch from the edge around the sewn edge. Lay the unsewn bottom of the collar along the top edge of the cape, matching the center of the collar to the center back of the cape, and making sure the collar ends are equidistant to the front opening on both sides. Pin and sew the collar to the cape. Remove the pins and press the seam, including the edges of the cape next to the collar, in along the wrong side of the cape. If you like, topstitch ¼ inch from the edge along the sewn edge. Trim the seams.

3. Have the child put on the cape and mark where to place the Velcro coins at the top of the cape's placket. Sew 2 loop (fuzzy) coins to the child's right side of the cape, facing out. Sew the hook (rough) Velcro to the left cape placket, facing in.

MATERIALS

2 yards red felt

red thread

6 red ¾-inch Velcro coins

6 inches ¾-inch-wide Velcro

about 6 ounces polyester fiberfill

TOOLS

patterns (see section at back of book)

BASE GARMENTS

red pants

red long sleeve shirt

HOOD

1. Using the hood pattern, cut out 4 pieces of felt. On each one, sew the dart seam closed (see the pattern), using a $1/4$-inch seam allowance. With right sides together, pin and then sew 2 pieces of felt from the back neck to the forehead, matching up the darts. Repeat for the lining, but leave a 3-inch opening in the back of the head seam to turn the whole hood right side out. Remove the pins.

2. With right sides together, pin the lining to the outside at the neck/back seam and at the forehead front seam. Pin all areas in between. Sew the lining to the hood, all the way around, using a $1/4$-inch seam allowance. Remove the pins.

3. Turn the hood right side out, by pulling through the hole. Hand stitch the hole closed. Topstitch $1/4$ inch all around the face opening, or iron it.

4. Sew 4 Velcro loop (fuzzy) coins in a square on the outside of the child's right flap. Sew two 3-inch strips of hook (rough) Velcro to the inside left flap.

5. Using the horn pattern, cut out 4 pieces of felt. Pin and then sew the pairs together, using $1/4$-inch seam allowances, leaving the base open. Remove the pins. Turn the horns right side out. Stuff with fiberfill. Pin the horns to the hood by matching their side seams to the dart seams and placing them equidistant from the center hood seam, about 2 inches down to either side. Hand sew securely in place. Remove the pins.

TAIL

1. Using the tail pattern, cut out 2 pieces of felt. Pin and then sew them together, using a $1/4$-inch seam allowance and leaving the upper end open and a hole in the side as marked on the pattern. Remove the pins. Turn the tail right side out. Stuff with fiberfill, using both openings. Hand stitch the side opening closed.

2. Pin the tail to the child's pants, about $1/2$ inch down from the waistband in the center of the back. Hand sew securely in place. Remove the pins.

fairy costume

Make a little girl's dream come true with this fairy princess outfit. If made directly from the pattern, this costume is a size 2/3. If you need a larger size, simply follow the instructions to adjust the fit. It can be adjusted to about a size 6 or 8.

SKIRT

1. For the waistband, measure the child around her waist. Add 8 inches. Cut a strip of purple felt that is 3 1/2 inches wide by this measurement long. Fold in half lengthwise; press.

2. From the child's waist, measure the length you want for the skirt. Add 3 inches. Lay the lavender crinoline out on a flat surface and cut 2 pieces the width of the crinoline by the skirt length. Sew the crinoline lengths together to make one approximately 200-inch-long strip. Repeat for the burgundy crinoline. Lay the burgundy strip on top of the lavender and sew together across the upper edge.

3. Using a double thickness of thread, sew 1/2-inch stitches right next to the stitching line across the entire top, pulling it to gather as you go along. Pull this gathering to match exactly the purple felt strip length. Slip the gathered fabric into the purple felt waistband. Pin in place. Sew the bottom and sides. Remove the pins.

4. Cut 3- or 4-inch scallops on the bottom of the lavender layer, all the way around. Repeat for the burgundy layer.

5. Sew two 3-inch strips of Velcro to the ends of the waistband, making sure that the hook (rough) side will face in and the loop (fuzzy) side will face out (this way the wings will not get caught on any exposed Velcro).

6. Using the leaf pattern, cut about 12 leaves from the fuchsia felt.

MATERIALS

1/2 yard purple felt

1 1/2 to 2 yards lavender crinoline (108 inches wide)

2 to 2 1/2 yards burgundy crinoline (108 inches wide)

lavender and burgundy thread

1 yard black 3/4-inch-wide Velcro

8- by 8-inch scrap fuchsia felt

small artificial purple and pink flowers

green and silver glitter

1/2 yard green felt

3/4 yard deep pink organza

1/2 yard 1/4-inch elastic

1 1/3 yards 2-inch-wide wired green ribbon

TOOLS

patterns (see section at back of book)

hot glue gun and sticks

fabric glue, such as Sobo Premium Craft and Fabric Glue

pinking shears

BASE GARMENTS

burgundy or purple leotard and tights

Reserve 6 to 8 artificial flowers for the headdress. Pull the remaining flowers off their stems and hot glue one to each leaf. Using the fabric glue, put a tiny bit on each leaf and sprinkle on some green glitter. Let dry, and then shake off the excess. Pin the flowers on the skirt in a random pattern and hand sew in place. Remove the pins.

VEST

1. Adjust the vest patterns: Measure the child from the shoulder (at the neck) to the waist. Add 2 inches and adjust the front and back patterns vertically to this measurement on the adjustment lines if necessary. Measure around the child's chest, divide this number by 2 and adjust the back at the adjustment line, to this measurement. Take the amount you increased the back, divide it in half, and add this amount to the front width at the adjustment line. Straighten out the shoulder lines. Don't adjust the neck or armholes until you cut out the pattern and sew it.

2. Use the adjusted pattern to cut out one back piece from the green felt. Cut out 4 front pieces: 2 green and 2 purple. Pin the green front pieces on top of the purple front pieces, making sure you have a left and a right side. Pin the back to the front at the shoulder seams, right sides together (that is, green fronts facing green back). Sew shoulder seams together. Remove the pins and try on the child. Adjust where necessary along the shoulder seam (make neck hole a little larger? Cut down width at arm?). See how the vest armholes will fit and mark where they should be cut a little larger if necessary. Remove the vest from the child and make the adjustments. Resew the shoulder seams if necessary. Pin and then sew the side seams. Remove the pins.

3. Place the vest on the child and mark with pins where the front overlaps. Remove from the child and attach the Velcro in the following way: On the child's right side of the vest, lift up the green pinned layer, and pin a 4-inch strip of Velcro on the purple felt layer, facing inside. On the other front side, pin the opposite Velcro on the green layer, facing outside. Sew these in place. Hot glue the 2 layers of front felt together where necessary.

4. With the fabric glue, squeeze out decorative swirling lines on one outer side of the vest front. Sprinkle with the green glitter and let dry. Repeat for the other side and let dry. Turn the vest over and make little dots with the glue, keeping decorations $1/2$ inch away from the shoulder seam and top of neck. Sprinkle with glitter and let dry.

5. Attach Velcro to the vest: Cut a 2-inch strip of loop (fuzzy) Velcro and pin it at neck center back. Measure across the shoulders and cut 2 more strips loop (rough) Velcro about $1/2$ inch shorter than the shoulders are wide and attach one to the back of each shoulder, about $1/4$ inch from the seam.

WINGS

1. Measure the child from the top of the spine at the neck to the wrist. Adjust the wing pattern so that the center back to the wrist is 2 inches longer than this measurement (for ease of movement). Make the pattern longer top to bottom, if desired.

2. Using this pattern and pinking shears, cut out a double layer of pink organza, aligning the fold with the fold mark on the pattern. Then cut out a double layer of burgundy crinoline, again aligning the folds. Sew the 2 pieces together across the top. Cut a purple felt strip, 1 inch wide by the length of the top, and pin it to the crinoline layer of the wing top. Sew together. Remove the pins.

3. Wrap the elastic around the child's wrist loosely enough to feel comfortable but not so loose as to fall off. Pin the ends where they meet and remove from the wrist. Sew as pinned and make a second one exactly the same. Attach one to each end of the felt strip at the top of the wings with a few stitches.

4. To attach the wings, take the 2-inch strip of hook (rough) Velcro that matches the Velcro at the vest center back and sew it onto the center of the felt strip on the wing. Put the vest on the child. Attach the Velcro loop strips that match the vest shoulders. Slip on the elastics at the wrists. At the child's shoulders, pin the wings to the vest. Remove the wings and vest, and pin the loop Velcro to the wings. Sew the Velcro in place. Remove the pins.

5. To decorate the wings, cut out eight 1½-inch purple felt circles. Make a fabric glue circle in the center of each and sprinkle on silver glitter. When dry, pin onto the crinoline layer of the wing. Have the child try on the wings. Correct the placement if necessary. Hand sew in place. Remove the pins.

HEADDRESS

1. Beginning in the center, sew the remaining artificial flowers onto the ribbon about 2½ inches apart. Gently place the ribbon around the child's head and twist to close it into a circle. Twist the dangling ends into ringlets that can droop down. Cut off ends if they are too long.

2. Make little dots on the ribbon with fabric glue and sprinkle with silver glitter. Let dry.

skeleton costume

On a dark Halloween night, whoever ventures out in this costume will scare everyone along the way! Let your trick-or-treater go rattling through the neighborhood—even the chilliest night won't bother this bag-o'-bones. Apply simple felt shapes to a black sweatsuit, and Mister or Miss Skeleton can stay outside in comfort.

1. Trace the skeleton bone pattern onto the white felt. Cut out.

2. Lay out the sweatshirt and pants and place the felt bones where appropriate. Measure the child so the elbow, shoulder, and knee joints are in the right places. Be sure to center the spine and ribcage. Pin the felt in place.

3. Glue the felt bones down carefully with the fabric glue. Remove the pins. Cut the finger tips off the black gloves.

4. To make the face paint, mix the cornstarch, cold cream, and water. Add food coloring, if you like. If making more than one color, mix each color in its own muffin tin cup or film canister. Stir until well blended.

5. With the small paintbrush, paint the child's face with the face paint, being careful to avoid the area around the eyes.

❖　❖　❖

MATERIALS

1 yard white felt

face paint: 1 teaspoon cornstarch, 1/2 teaspoon cold cream, 1/2 teaspoon water

food coloring (optional)

TOOLS

pattern (see section at back of book)

life-size Halloween skeleton decoration (available in party-supply stores)

fabric glue, such as Sobo Premium Craft and Fabric Glue

small paintbrush

BASE GARMENTS

black sweatshirt

black sweatpants

black stretch one-size-fits-all gloves

tip
If you would like to wash and reuse this costume, sew the felt onto the sweats. You might find this easier to do if you open up the side seams of the sleeves and pants. After the felt has been sewn on, close up these seams.

red riding hood
costume

Inspired by the favorite Grimm's fairy tale, this costume will turn any little girl into a dutiful granddaughter carrying provisions through the forest. Just add a wolf and the picture is complete. This costume is a size 6/8. You can make all or parts of it—the cape would work well in any color or pattern (say, in black for Zorro, or blue for a superhero).

HOODED CAPE

1. Measure from the child's shoulder to the knee and adjust the cape pattern so that its full length comes to several inches below the knee. Using this pattern, cut out a double layer of red felt, aligning the fold with the fold mark on the pattern. Using the hood pattern, cut out 2 pieces of red felt. Using the hood facing pattern, cut out 2 pieces of red felt.

2. Pin and sew the back and top seams of the hood together, using a $1/2$-inch seam allowance. Pin and sew the top of the facing pieces together, using a $1/2$-inch seam allowance. Remove the pins. Iron open the seams.

3. Match the front of the facing to the front of the hood and pin in place, making sure the seams match up and the right sides are together. Sew a $1/4$-inch seam. Remove the pins. Press the seam open. Fold the facing in along this seam and pin to the inside of the hood. Sew the facing in place. Remove the pins. Turn the hood right side out again. Turn the facing/hood front edge back to the notch on the hood at the neck. Pin in place.

4. Pin the hood to the cape, right sides together, matching up the hood back seam with the cape center back notch. Make sure the hood

MATERIALS

2 $1/2$ yards red felt
(60 inches wide)

red and white thread

4 red $3/4$-inch Velcro coins

1 yard white felt

1 yard $3/4$-inch-wide white Velcro

red acrylic or fabric paint

blue fabric marker

TOOLS

patterns (see section at back of book)

stencil brush

paring knife

potato

BASE GARMENTS

blue cotton knit dress

red tights

opening is equidistant on both sides of the front cape opening. Sew the hood to the cape, using a $1/2$-inch seam allowance, and securing the folded-back facing/hood edge. Stitch down the seam allowance to the cape neck.

5. Fold in both sides of the cape front $1/2$ inch and sew down.

6. On the the child's right side of the cape, on the inside along the folded-in edge, pin and sew a line of 4 hook (rough) red Velcro coins, starting at the top and evenly spaced about every 2 inches. Pin and sew the loop (fuzzy) Velcro to the outside of the left side.

APRON

1. For the waistband, measure the child around her waist. Add 8 inches. Cut a strip from the white felt that is $3\,1/2$ inches wide by this measurement long.

2. Using the bib pattern, cut out one piece of white felt. Using the back strap pattern, cut 2 pieces of white felt. Sew the straps to the bib front at the shoulder seams, using a $1/2$-inch seam allowance. Sew down the seam allowance.

3. Using the apron skirt pattern, cut out one piece of white felt. Make a small notch at the center front top.

4. Hand sew 2 parallel lines of stitches $\frac{1}{2}$ inch apart along the top of the apron skirt. Gather the top of the apron skirt until it is about 4 inches wider than the bottom of the bib front. Pin the center top of the apron skirt to the center bottom of the white felt waistband. Matching edges, pin in place and sew together, using a $\frac{1}{2}$-inch seam allowance. Pin the bottom of the bib to the apron/waistband seam, wrong sides facing, matching at center front. Sew in place. Bring the bib front up so it looks like an apron. Pin the waistband in place on top of the bib front and sew it down. Sew the excess seam allowance for the apron skirt up against the waistband on the inside.

5. Attach the white Velcro as follows: Cut 2 hook (rough) strips 6 inches long and attach to the inside of the back straps at the base where they will meet up with the waistband. Cut 2 loop (fuzzy) strips 8 inches long and pin to the outside of one end of the waistband, one above the other horizontally. Sew in place. Cut 2 hook (rough) strips 8 inches long and attach on the other side of the fabric, to the wrong side of the waistband. You can sew them right on the same stitching lines. And finally, cut 2 loop (fuzzy) strips 8 inches long and attach these, one above the other, on the outside of the other end of the waistband.

PAINTING THE DRESS AND APRON

1. Using the stencil brush, paint red polka dots onto the dress skirt.

2. Using the blue fabric marker, draw vertical blue stripes, about 2 inches apart, on the bib front, back straps, waist band, and apron skirt.

3. Using the paring knife, cut the potato in half and then draw a flower, 1 to 1 $\frac{1}{2}$ inches wide, on one of the halves. Cut away the excess potato around the flower shape. Apply red paint to it and stamp flowers in between the blue lines. This will be a little tricky where the apron is gathered to the waistband, but it is possible to smooth it long enough to print. With the fabric marker, put blue dots in the middle of each flower.

lion costume

The hooded sweatshirt and sweatpants of this easy-to-make costume will keep a child warm, making this a good choice for a cold October 31.

1. Using the tail pattern, cut out 2 pieces of tan felt. Pin the 2 pieces together, then sew, using a $1/2$-inch seam allowance and being sure to leave holes open as marked on pattern. Remove the pins.

2. Stuff the tail with fiberfill, using both holes. Hand sew the side hole closed. Pin the tail to the back of the pants, $1/2$ inch below the waistband. Hand sew in place. Remove the pins.

3. Using the tail tip pattern, cut 2 pieces of the fuzzy light tan felt. Pin one piece around the tail, 4 inches up from the bottom end. Pin the second piece overlapping the other so the tail is completely encircled. Hand sew in place. Remove the pins.

4. Using the tail tip fringe pattern, cut out 8 pieces of felt—2 tan, 2 fuzzy light tan, 2 yellow, and 2 gold. Using the tail tip strip pattern, cut out one piece of tan felt. Lay the strip down flat and place the fringe strips on it perpendicularly, lining them up along the strip. Pin and then sew in place. Remove the pins. Wrap this strip around the top of the lion tail tip with the fringe going toward the tail end and hand sew in place. You may want to put a few tacking stitches into the tail tip itself.

5. Using all the felt colors, cut at least 100 strips $1/2$ inch wide by 12 to 15 inches long. Measure around the opening of the sweatshirt hood. Add 4 inches. Cut a strip of tan felt, 2 inches wide by this measurement long. Lay this hood strip down on a flat surface and lay the $1/2$-inch strips across it, alternating the colors and having differing

MATERIALS

$1/3$ yard tan felt

tan and yellow thread

about 6 ounces polyester fiberfill

$1/3$ yard fuzzy light tan felt

$1/3$ yard yellow felt

$1/3$ yard gold felt

2 yards transparent fishing line (optional)

1 foot $1/4$-inch elastic (optional)

TOOLS

patterns (see section at back of book)

hot glue gun and sticks

BASE GARMENTS

yellow sweatpants

yellow hooded zip-up sweatshirt

tan one-size-fits-all gloves

lengths on each side of the strip. Be sure that there is an even distribution of strips along the hood strip. Pin the strips in place and then sew to the hood strip, about $1/4$ inch from one edge. Remove the pins.

6. Pin the center of the hood strip to the center front of the outside of the sweatshirt hood. Pin around each side and let the 2 inches at each end dangle down at the neck line. Sew the strip to the hood, being careful to sew only the strip, not the fringe pieces. Remove the pins.

7. Have the child put the sweatshirt on. Trim the strips at the top so his face shows well enough and he can see, or tack any wayward strips to the hood.

8. To make the talons, use the talon pattern to cut out 10 pieces of fuzzy light tan felt and 10 of yellow felt. Hot glue a yellow one to each finger of the gloves on the palm side, $1/2$ inch from the tip. Turn the gloves over and repeat with tan on the outer side, then glue the tan and yellow felt together where they touch.

9. If you like, sew or tie fishing line to the tail tip and tie on an elastic loop for the child to wear around his wrist and manipulate the tail like a puppet. Adjust the length of the fishing line, as necessary.

witch costume

Look who just flew in—the patchwork witch! Make the creation of this costume a joint venture: witches-to-be will take great pride in deciding where the patches will go, and then helping to sew them on. Don't mind if little fingers make big stitches, the ragtag look is in style these days. And don't forget the broom— there's no better way to fly around the neighborhood. This makes a very loose, roomy size 6.

DRESS

1. Using the patterns, cut out 2 body pieces and 2 sleeve pieces from the black knit. For the front of the dress, cut the neck opening of one body piece $1\frac{1}{2}$ inches deeper, keeping it the same width at the shoulders (see pattern).

2. Pin the dress front and back together at shoulder seams, right sides together. Sew together using a $\frac{1}{2}$-inch seam allowance. Remove the pins. Open up, right side facing up, and pin the sleeves in place, right sides together, matching the shoulder seam to the shoulder notch. Sew the armhole seam. Fold the garment, right sides together, along the shoulder seams. Pin the side seams together, including the sleeve seam, and sew closed. Remove the pins. Turn right side out.

3. Cut triangles of varying sizes out of the dress bottom and sleeve ends, for a slightly ragged look. Pin some of the triangles together, overlapping each triangle about $\frac{1}{2}$ inch onto the next one, and create a strip that equals the circumference of the neck opening. Sew the triangles together and remove the pins. Pin this strip along the wrong side of the neck opening and sew it $\frac{1}{4}$ inch from the neck edge. Turn it right side out and top stitch it down $\frac{1}{4}$ inch from the edge.

MATERIALS

$2\frac{1}{2}$ yards black stretch knit fabric

scrap black and white print fabric

scraps blue and red felt

$\frac{3}{4}$ yard black felt

18- by 18-inch piece flat corrugated cardboard

TOOLS

patterns (see section at back of book)

pinking shears

compass

fabric and paper spray adhesive, such as S704 Fabric and Foam Adhesive from BFG Goodrich

X-Acto knife

4-inch diameter shipping tube

royal blue and red fabric markers

BASE GARMENTS

white tights

black turtleneck sweater

4. For the patches, cut squares and rectangles from the scrap pieces, using the pinking shears and regular scissors. Put a few aside to add to the hat. Place the remaining patches randomly on the dress, pin in place, and sew down. Cut out one triangle piece from the felt and sew it onto collar. Remove the pins.

HAT AND TIGHTS

1. Using the cone pattern, cut one piece of black felt. Pin the 2 straight edges to each other, and sew together using a $\frac{1}{2}$-inch seam allowance. Remove the pins. Clip off excess at top and turn right side out. Place on child's head and mark where the cone fits. Cut $\frac{1}{4}$ inch below this line.

2. Cut out 2 layers of black felt using the brim pattern. Center the cone on top of the brim pattern. Carefully mark the cone circle on the pattern. Remove the cone. Cut out the inner circle from the pattern. Place the pattern on the corrugated cardboard and trace the outer and inner circles. With the compass, draw another circle 1 inch smaller than the outer circle. With the X-Acto knife, cut the cardboard there. Draw a circle $\frac{1}{4}$ inch bigger than the inner circle. Cut there.

3. Spray adhesive on one side of the corrugated cardboard and one circle of the felt. Carefully center the corrugated cardboard on the felt. Repeat with the other side of the cardboard and the other piece of felt. Lay the brim pattern on the brim and trace the inner hole. Cut pie slices into the felt from the center out to this traced line. Place the cone on the brim, with the pie slices on the inside of the cone. Pin in a few places and try on the child. If the hat needs to be larger, make the pie slice cuts a little deeper and slightly stretch the cone felt if necessary. If it needs to be smaller, you can fix that later.

4. Now unpin, and spray adhesive onto the pie slices to glue inside the hat (use the brim pattern paper to cover the parts of the hat you don't want sprayed). Also spray the bottom 2 inches of the cone. When tacky, attach the glued pieces.

5. Cut a 2- by 26-inch strip of black felt and wrap it around the base of the cone to form a hat band, overlapping the excess. Sew or glue in place. If the hat was too big, layer strips of felt around the inner circumference of the hat opening to make it smaller. Glue or sew in place.

6. Sew a few patches randomly on the hat. Trim the outer brim with pinking shears.

7. Insert the shipping tube into one leg of the tights. Use the blue marker to make horizontal stripes by drawing parallel circles, about $\frac{3}{4}$ inch apart, around the leg. Let dry. Repeat with the other leg, using the red marker.

recipes

PINEAPPLE-GLAZED HAM

More than enough to feed a ghoulish crowd, this ham can be the centerpiece of a buffet at a large, spooky party or open house. Kids will love the pineapple glaze, which is not too sweet for adults.

> 1 12- to 14-pound fully-cooked smoked ham
> whole cloves
> 1 10-ounce jar pineapple preserves
> 1 tablespoon brown prepared mustard
> 1 1/2 8-ounce cans pineapple slices, drained
> mint sprigs

1. Heat the oven to 325°F. Remove the skin and excess fat from the ham, leaving a layer of fat about 1/4 inch thick. Score the fat layer into diamonds and insert a clove in the center of each diamond. Place the ham in a roasting pan. Bake 1 1/2 hours.

2. In a small bowl, combine the preserves and mustard; brush 1 or 2 tablespoons over the ham. Make one cut through each pineapple slice. Place the pineapple on the ham, interlocking the slices to make a chain. Bake the ham 1 hour longer, brushing with the glaze often. Transfer the ham to a carving board and garnish with mint sprigs.

MAKES 20 OR MORE SERVINGS

SPICY THREE-BEAN CHILI

This super-quick version of the all-American favorite is a warming dish for hungry goblins returning from trick-or-treating. Go easy on the hot red-pepper sauce if you're feeding pint-sized party-goers.

> 2 tablespoons vegetable oil
> 2 medium-size onions, coarsely chopped
> 3 cloves garlic, finely chopped
> 2 28-ounce cans crushed tomatoes
> 2 16-ounce cans red kidney beans, undrained
> 2 16-ounce cans black beans, undrained
> 1 16-ounce can chickpeas, undrained
> 2 tablespoons ground cumin
> 1 to 2 tablespoons chili powder
> 1 to 2 tablespoons hot red-pepper sauce
> 1/2 teaspoon ground black pepper
> hot rice or warm corn tortillas

Heat the oil in a 5-quart saucepan or Dutch oven over medium heat. Add the onions and garlic; sauté 10 to 15 minutes, or until the onions are golden. Stir in the tomatoes, kidney beans, black beans, chickpeas, cumin, chile powder, red-pepper sauce, and black pepper. Heat to boiling. Serve over rice or with warm tortillas.

MAKES ABOUT 12 SERVINGS

PUMPKIN BISQUE

Get into the spirit of the holiday with this creamy, richly colored soup. Pumpkin is the star, adding flavor, body, and a beautiful terra-cotta color. Serve with dark rye bread for the full Halloween effect.

1 tablespoon butter

1 medium-size onion, chopped

1 stalk celery, chopped

1 medium-size carrot, peeled and chopped

1 medium-size potato, peeled and chopped

1 clove garlic, chopped

4 1/2 cups water

1 teaspoon salt

1 16-ounce can pumpkin puree

1/4 cup honey

1 tablespoon chopped peeled fresh gingerroot

1 cup milk

1. In a 4-quart saucepan, melt the butter over medium heat. Add the onion, celery, carrot, and potato, and sauté 5 minutes. Add the garlic and sauté 5 minutes longer. Stir in the water and salt; heat to boiling. Reduce the heat to low, cover, and simmer 30 minutes.

2. Stir the pumpkin, honey, and gingerroot into the soup; cook, uncovered and stirring occasionally, 20 minutes. Stir in the milk.

3. In batches, transfer the soup to a blender and puree. Transfer to a clean saucepan and gently reheat. Serve immediately.

MAKES 6 TO 8 SERVINGS

STUFFED SUGAR PUMPKIN

Be sure to get an eating pumpkin (called pie, sweet, or sugar pumpkin) for this savory treat; jack-o'-lantern pumpkins are not very tasty. Save the seeds to make Roasted Pumpkin Seeds (page 96).

1 1/2 cups water

1/2 cup wild rice

1 teaspoon salt

1 4- to 5-pound sugar or other eating pumpkin

2 teaspoons vegetable oil

1 pound ground venison or lean ground beef

1/2 cup chopped green onions

1 teaspoon crushed dried sage

1/4 teaspoon pepper

1. In a 1-quart saucepan, heat the water to boiling over high heat. Stir in the wild rice and 1/2 teaspoon salt. Return to boiling. Cover; reduce the heat to low, and cook 40 to 45 minutes, or until the rice is tender and all the water is absorbed.

2. Heat the oven to 350°F. Cut the top off the pumpkin and discard. Remove the seeds and fibers from the center. Save the seeds for roasting or discard. Set the pumpkin in 1/2 inch of water in a shallow roasting pan.

3. In a large skillet, heat the oil over medium-high heat. Add the venison and sauté until browned. Remove the skillet from the heat. Stir in the cooked wild rice, all but 1 tablespoon of the green onions, the sage, the

remaining $1/2$ teaspoon salt, and the pepper. Spoon the meat mixture into the pumpkin and cover the top with aluminum foil.

4. Bake the stuffed pumpkin 45 to 60 minutes, or until tender when pierced with a fork. During baking, add more water to the roasting pan if necessary to keep the pumpkin from sticking.

5. Transfer the pumpkin to a serving dish; remove the foil and sprinkle with the remaining 1 tablespoon green onions. To serve, cut the pumpkin into wedges. Place a wedge with stuffing on each plate.

MAKES **6** SERVINGS

MAPLE-PECAN SWEET POTATOES

A beautiful amber glaze coats golden chunks of sweet potato.

> 8 medium-size (about 3$1/2$ pounds) sweet potatoes, peeled and cut into 1$1/2$-inch chunks
> $1/2$ cup firmly packed light brown sugar
> $1/3$ cup maple syrup
> $1/4$ cup ($1/2$ stick) butter or margarine
> $1/4$ teaspoon salt
> $1/8$ teaspoon ground black pepper
> $1/4$ cup pecan halves, toasted

1. Cook the sweet potatoes in a large saucepan of boiling water about 20 minutes, or until tender. Drain well.

2. Meanwhile, in a 1-quart saucepan, combine the brown sugar, maple syrup, butter, salt, and pepper. Heat to boiling over medium-high heat. Reduce the heat to low. Cook, stirring constantly, about 2 minutes, or until clear and thickened.

3. Transfer the potatoes to a serving dish, top with the syrup mixture, sprinkle with the pecans, and serve.

MAKES **8** SERVINGS

CARROT-RAISIN SALAD WITH TOASTED WALNUTS

You won't have any trouble getting the kids to eat this salad—it's all dressed up in the spooky colors of the day! Serve cold or at room temperature. Double the recipe if you are expecting a lot of guests.

> $3/4$ cup orange juice
> $1/4$ cup walnut or vegetable oil
> 1 tablespoon honey
> $1/4$ teaspoon salt
> 1$1/2$ pounds carrots, peeled and coarsely shredded
> $3/4$ cup dark seedless raisins
> $2/3$ cup walnuts, coarsely chopped and toasted

In a medium-size bowl, with a wire whisk, beat together the orange juice, oil, honey, and salt. Stir the carrots, raisins, and walnuts into the dressing. Refrigerate, covered, several hours or overnight. Toss just before serving.

MAKES **6** SERVINGS

MARINATED VEGETABLE SALAD

This piquant melange of olives, cauliflower, and carrots, a bit more adult than the Carrot-Raisin Salad (page 95), also features the colors of the day. It's an ideal make-ahead party dish since the flavor improves when it is refrigerated overnight.

> 1 pound carrots, peeled and cut into 3- by
>   1/2-inch sticks
>
> 1 large head (2 1/2 pounds) cauliflower, trimmed
>   and cut into small flowerets
>
> 1/2 cup extra-virgin olive oil
>
> 1/4 cup red wine vinegar
>
> 1/3 cup chopped fresh parsley leaves, plus sprigs for
>   garnish
>
> 1 teaspoon sugar
>
> 3/4 teaspoon salt
>
> 1/2 teaspoon dry mustard
>
> 1/4 teaspoon ground black pepper
>
> 1 cup mixed brine-cured green and ripe olives

1. In a 5-quart saucepan, heat 2 inches water to boiling over high heat. Add the carrots and return the water to boiling. Add the cauliflower and cook 10 to 15 minutes, or just until the carrots and cauliflower are tender-crisp. Drain and rinse with cold water; set aside in a large bowl.

2. For the marinade, in a jar with a tight-fitting lid, combine the oil, vinegar, chopped parsley, sugar, salt, mustard, and pepper until well mixed. Pour over the vegetables and toss. Cover and refrigerate 2 hours or overnight, stirring occasionally.

3. Just before serving, add the olives to the salad and toss until well mixed. Spoon into a serving bowl, garnish with parsley sprigs, and serve.

MAKES **12** SERVINGS

ROASTED PUMPKIN SEEDS

Don't throw out those seeds when carving a jack-o'-lantern (page 59) or making Stuffed Sugar Pumpkins (page 94): They make a wonderful, crunchy snack. If you have more than one cup of seeds, simply multiply the oil and salt accordingly.

> 1 cup raw pumpkin seeds, separated from fibers
>
> 1 teaspoon olive or corn oil
>
> 1/4 teaspoon salt

1. Heat the oven to 350°F. Rub the pumpkin seeds in a cloth towel to separate them from any remaining fibers.

2. On a rimmed baking sheet, combine the seeds, oil, and salt. Spread out in a single layer. Bake 10 to 15 minutes, or until the seeds are dry and just beginning to brown. Let cool and serve.

MAKES **1** CUP

SUGAR-AND-SPICE ALMONDS

Place these nibbles in small bowls around the house at Halloween—adults and kids alike will gobble them up.

1/3 cup sugar

4 teaspoons ground cinnamon

1/2 teaspoon ground nutmeg

2 cups natural whole almonds

3 tablespoons light corn syrup

1. Heat the oven to 350°F. Coat a rimmed baking sheet with nonstick cooking spray.

2. In a cup or small bowl, combine the sugar, cinnamon, and nutmeg; set aside. In a medium-size bowl, stir together the almonds and corn syrup until the almonds are well coated.

3. Add the sugar mixture to the almond mixture, stirring until well combined. Spread on the greased baking sheet and bake about 10 minutes, or until the sugar coating is bubbly and the almonds are browned.

4. Let cool on the baking sheet to room temperature, stirring occasionally to prevent sticking and to separate the almonds. Store in an airtight container.

MAKES ABOUT 2 CUPS

MAPLE POPCORN

Serve this traditional American treat shortly after it is made, while it is at its crisp best.

1/3 cup unpopped popcorn

2/3 cup sugar

2/3 cup water

1/8 teaspoon cream of tartar

2/3 cup maple syrup

2 tablespoons butter

1/2 teaspoon salt

1. Pop the popcorn in a hot air popper into a large bowl. Generously grease a baking sheet.

2. In 2-quart saucepan, heat the sugar, water, and cream of tartar to boiling over high heat, stirring occasionally. Brush the side of the pan with warm water to dissolve any crystals forming at the edge. Reduce the heat to medium and continue cooking, without stirring, about 10 minutes, or until the mixture becomes a deep golden brown.

3. Carefully stir in the maple syrup and cook 2 minutes longer. Remove from heat. Stir in the butter and salt until the butter melts. Immediately pour the sugar mixture over the popcorn: With a long-handled spoon, carefully stir the popcorn to coat thoroughly with the sugar mixture (do not use your hands; the syrup is very hot). Pour onto the greased baking sheet to cool. Serve when cool.

MAKES ABOUT 2 QUARTS

AUTUMN FRUIT PIE

Celebrate the harvest with this flavorful offering. Dates impart a natural sweetness to a generous apple filling, while cranberries lend a balancing tart flavor and rosy color.

PASTRY

> 2 cups unsifted all-purpose flour
>
> 1/2 teaspoon salt
>
> 1/2 cup (1 stick) butter
>
> 1/4 cup vegetable shortening
>
> 4 to 5 tablespoons cold water

AUTUMN FRUIT FILLING

> 10 Granny Smith apples, peeled, cored, and thinly sliced
>
> 1 cup pitted dates, chopped
>
> 1 cup fresh cranberries
>
> 1/2 cup sugar
>
> 1 tablespoon lemon juice
>
> 1 teaspoon ground cinnamon
>
> 1/4 teaspoon ground nutmeg

1. Prepare the pastry: In a medium-size bowl, combine the flour and salt. With a pastry blender or 2 knives, cut the butter and shortening into the flour mixture until the mixture resembles coarse crumbs. One tablespoon at a time, sprinkle the water over the flour mixture and mix lightly until the pastry holds together when lightly pressed. Shape the pastry into 2 equal balls and flatten each to a 1-inch thickness. Wrap and refrigerate for 30 minutes.

2. Prepare the Autumn Fruit Filling: In a 5-quart saucepan, combine the apples, dates, cranberries, sugar, lemon juice, cinnamon, and nutmeg. Heat to boiling over medium heat, stirring frequently. Cook about 20 minutes, or until the apples are soft but still retain their shape.

3. Heat the oven to 400°F. Between 2 sheets of floured waxed paper, roll out one ball of pastry to an 11-inch round. Remove the top sheet of paper and invert the pastry onto a 9-inch pie plate, letting excess extend over the edge. Remove the remaining sheet of waxed paper. Spoon the apple filling onto the pastry.

4. Roll out the remaining pastry to a 12-inch round to make the top crust. Remove the top sheet of paper and invert the pastry over the filling. Remove the paper; gently press the pastries around the rim where they meet. Carefully fold the edge of the top crust under the edge of the bottom crust, making a soft rolled border that is even with the rim of the plate. Cut 4 slits in the top to allow steam to escape during baking.

5. Bake the pie 30 to 35 minutes, or until the pastry is golden brown. Cool on a wire rack 15 to 20 minutes before serving.

MAKES 10 SERVINGS

PUMPKIN CHEESECAKE

A great do-ahead Halloween dessert, this treat can be made the day before the party.

GINGERSNAP CRUST

- 1/3 cup butter or margarine
- 1 1/2 cups gingersnap cookie crumbs

PUMPKIN CHEESE FILLING

- 2 8-ounce packages cream cheese, softened
- 1/2 cup sugar
- 1/2 cup canned pumpkin puree or cooked pumpkin puree
- 1/2 teaspoon ground cinnamon
- 1/4 teaspoon ground cloves
- 1/4 teaspoon ground nutmeg
- 2 large eggs
- 1/2 teaspoon vanilla extract

1. Prepare the Gingersnap Crust: In a small saucepan, melt the butter over low heat. Remove from heat and stir in the cookie crumbs until well mixed. Press the mixture firmly onto the bottom of a 9-inch spring-form pan and set aside.

2. Heat the oven to 350°F. Prepare the Pumpkin Cheese Filling: In a large bowl, with an electric mixer on medium speed, beat the cream cheese, sugar, pumpkin, cinnamon, cloves, and nutmeg until combined. Beat in the eggs and vanilla until well mixed. Pour into the crust.

3. Bake 40 to 45 minutes, or until the center is almost set. Cool on a wire rack to room temperature. Cover and refrigerate 3 hours or overnight.

4. Just before serving, remove the rim of the pan and place the cheesecake on a serving plate.

MAKES **8** SERVINGS

MARBLED BROWNIES

While these are a good choice to take to a neighborhood Halloween party, they smell so good baking that it is only fair to make another pan for your family.

- 3 ounces unsweetened chocolate
- 1/4 cup (1/2 stick) butter or margarine
- 1 8-ounce package cream cheese, softened
- 1 cup sugar
- 1 tablespoon cornstarch
- 3 large eggs
- 1/4 teaspoon almond extract
- 1/2 cup unsifted all-purpose flour
- 1 teaspoon vanilla extract
- 1/2 teaspoon baking powder
- 1/4 teaspoon salt
- 1/2 cup finely chopped walnuts

1. Heat the oven to 350°F. Grease a 9-inch-square pan. Melt the chocolate and butter in a small saucepan over low heat; let cool to room temperature.

2. In a small bowl, beat the cream cheese with an electric mixer until fluffy. Gradually beat in 1/4 cup sugar, the cornstarch, 1 egg, and the

almond extract. Beat until smooth; set aside.

3. Wash and dry the beaters. In a medium-size bowl, beat the remaining 2 eggs until thick. Gradually beat in the remaining ¾ cup sugar. At low speed, beat in the chocolate mixture, flour, vanilla, baking powder, and salt. With a spoon, stir in the walnuts.

4. Spread half the chocolate mixture in the greased pan. Spread the cream cheese mixture over the top. Spoon dollops of the remaining chocolate mixture on top. With a spoon, swirl the batters together slightly to marbleize.

5. Bake 40 minutes, or until firm. Cool in the pan on a wire rack 10 minutes. Cut into squares. Cool completely. Wrap in plastic wrap; store in the refrigerator.

MAKES **16** BROWNIES

HALLOWEEN COOKIES

Create a spooky parade of jack-o'-lantern cookies with pumpkin cookie cutters. Meringue powder, specialty cookie cutters, and paste food coloring (which is more intense than liquid coloring) are available at cake decorating stores, or by mail order from Wilton Industries, 800-794-5866.

¾ cup granulated sugar

½ cup (1 stick) butter, softened

1 large egg

1 teaspoon vanilla extract

2 cups unsifted all-purpose flour

¼ teaspoon baking powder

¼ teaspoon salt

ROYAL ICING

1 1-pound package (3½ cups) confectioners' sugar

3 large egg whites or equivalent amount of meringue powder

½ teaspoon cream of tartar

orange, green, and black paste food coloring

1. In a medium-size bowl, with an electric mixer on medium speed, beat the granulated sugar and butter until light and fluffy. Beat in the egg and vanilla until well mixed. Reduce the speed to low and gradually beat in the flour, baking powder, and salt. Gather dough into a ball, flatten into a 5-inch round, and wrap in plastic wrap. Refrigerate dough at least 30 minutes or overnight.

2. Heat the oven to 325°F. Lightly grease 2 baking sheets. Cut 2 pieces of waxed paper the same size as the baking sheets. Cut the dough round in half. Wrap and return one piece to the refrigerator.

3. Lightly flour the waxed paper and roll out the dough between the paper to an ⅛-inch thickness. Remove the top piece of waxed paper from the dough. With different sizes of pumpkin cookie cutters, cut out as many cookies as possible, leaving at least a ½-inch space between them. Remove the trimmings and press together to reuse. Invert the

waxed paper with the shapes onto a greased baking sheet. Peel off the waxed paper. Reroll the dough trimmings between the floured waxed paper and cut out more shapes. Invert the paper onto the second baking sheet; peel off the paper.

4. Bake the cookies 10 to 14 minutes (depending on size) or until just golden at the edges. Cool 5 minutes on the baking sheets; transfer to wire racks and cool completely.

5. Repeat Steps 3 and 4 with the remaining dough, using additional sheets of waxed paper, if necessary.

6. Prepare the Royal Icing: In a large bowl, with an electric mixer on low speed, beat the confectioners' sugar, egg whites, and cream of tartar until mixed. Increase the speed to high and beat about 5 minutes, or until very thick and fluffy. Cover tightly with plastic wrap to prevent drying until ready to use.

7. Transfer some of the frosting to 2 small bowls and color with the black and green food coloring. Cover with plastic wrap. Color the remaining frosting orange. Transfer some of the orange frosting to a medium-size bowl and beat in a few teaspoons of water, until it reaches a spreadable consistency.

8. Spread the orange frosting on the cooled cookies with the back of a spoon. Let dry completely.

9. Transfer the orange frosting in the large bowl to a pastry bag fitted with a #1 tip. Use to pipe lines and dots on the cookies, leaving space in the middle of some to make jack-o'-lantern faces.

10. Repeat Step 9 with the green and black frosting, making stems and facial features.

MAKES **2** TO **3** DOZEN COOKIES

CANDY ACORNS

These whimsical acorn-shaped caramels are a delicious way to jazz up your Halloween decor. Scatter them around the serving dishes on the buffet table or use to fill small bowls around the room. Melted chocolate chips make the "caps" for the acorns.

1 14-ounce can sweetened condensed milk (not evaporated milk)

1 cup light corn syrup

1/8 teaspoon salt

1 teaspoon vanilla extract

1/2 cup semisweet chocolate chips

1/2 cup finely chopped walnuts

1. Line the bottom and 2 sides of an 8-inch-square baking pan with aluminum foil. Butter the foil on the bottom of the pan; set aside.

2. In a heavy 1 1/2-quart saucepan, heat the condensed milk, corn syrup, and salt over medium heat to boiling, stirring constantly. Continue to cook and stir over medium-low heat 15 to 20 minutes, or until the mixture thickens and the temperature reaches 238°F on a candy thermometer, or the soft-ball stage. Remove from heat and stir in the vanilla. Pour into the prepared pan, spreading evenly. Cool in the pan on a wire rack just until firm enough to cut.

3. Lift the candy from the pan and peel off the foil. Cut the candy into 1-inch pieces.

Shape each into an acorn, with one end slightly wider and flatter than the other. Place on a tray and refrigerate until firm.

4. Place the chocolate chips in a cup and set in a small saucepan with 1 inch of hot water. Place the pan over medium heat and melt the chocolate until smooth. Remove the cup from the pan. Dip the flat end of each caramel acorn into the chocolate, then into the walnuts. Let the chocolate set. Store the candies in a single layer in a container in the refrigerator.

MAKES ABOUT **5** DOZEN

CAKE DOUGHNUTS

To make tender doughnuts, pat the dough scraps together instead of re-rolling them. Offer both sugar doughnuts and cinnamon versions to your guests.

3 cups unsifted all-purpose flour

1 cup sugar

1 tablespoon baking powder

1 1/2 teaspoons ground cinnamon

1/2 teaspoon salt

1/4 teaspoon ground nutmeg

1 cup milk

1 large egg

1/4 cup (1/2 stick) butter or margarine, melted

vegetable oil for frying

1. In a large bowl, combine the flour, 1/2 cup sugar, the baking powder, 1 teaspoon cinna-

mon, the salt, and nutmeg. In a small bowl, combine the milk, egg, and butter. Stir the milk mixture into the flour mixture until well combined. Cover and refrigerate the dough at least 1 hour.

2. On a well-floured board, with a floured rolling pin, roll out the dough to a 1/2-inch thickness. Using a lightly floured 3-inch doughnut cutter with center in place, cut out doughnuts and holes. Pat the scraps together to form 3-inch rounds and cut with the doughnut cutter.

3. In a 3-quart saucepan, heat 2 inches vegetable oil to 370°F. Fry the doughnuts and holes, a few at a time, turning often, 2 to 3 minutes, or until golden brown. Drain on paper towels.

4. In a small plastic or paper bag, combine 1/4 cup sugar and the remaining 1/2 teaspoon cinnamon. Put the remaining 1/4 cup sugar into another bag. Toss half the doughnuts and holes, a few at a time, in the bag to coat with the cinnamon sugar mixture. Toss the remaining doughnuts and holes in the sugar.

MAKES ABOUT 16 DOUGHNUTS AND 16 HOLES

MULLED CIDER

Nothing could be simpler, or more warming on a blustery night, than apple cider, quickly heated and spiced. Before guests arrive, fill your home with a warm autumnal scent by heating this on the stove.

8 cups (1/2 gallon) apple cider

1 tablespoon whole allspice

1 tablespoon whole cloves

8 long cinnamon sticks

In a 3-quart saucepan, heat the cider, allspice, cloves, and cinnamon to boiling. With tongs, place a cinnamon stick in each of 8 mugs. Strain hot cider into mugs and serve.

MAKES 8 SERVINGS

SPARKLING SPICED CRANBERRY PUNCH

Light and refreshing, fit for a crowd.

2 cups water

1/2 cup sugar

4 3-inch cinnamon sticks

1/2 teaspoon whole cloves

ice cubes

2 8 1/2-ounce packages liquid concentrated cranberry juice cocktail

2 1-liter bottles seltzer, chilled

1. In a 2-quart saucepan over high heat, heat the water, sugar, cinnamon, and cloves to boiling. Remove from heat; let stand 15 minutes. Cover and refrigerate until cold.

2. Just before serving, strain the spice mixture over ice cubes into a small punch bowl. Add the cranberry juice concentrate and mix well. Stir in the seltzer and serve.

MAKES ABOUT 13 CUPS OR 16 SERVINGS

pillow patterns

SEE PAGE **46** FOR INSTRUCTIONS

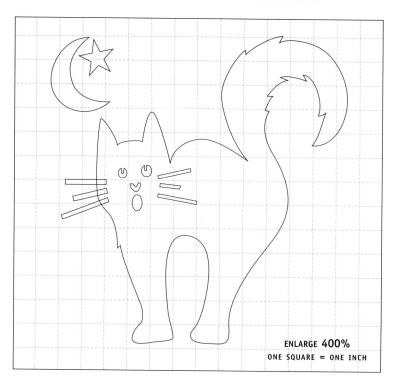

ENLARGE **400%**
ONE SQUARE = ONE INCH

ENLARGE **400%**
ONE SQUARE = ONE INCH

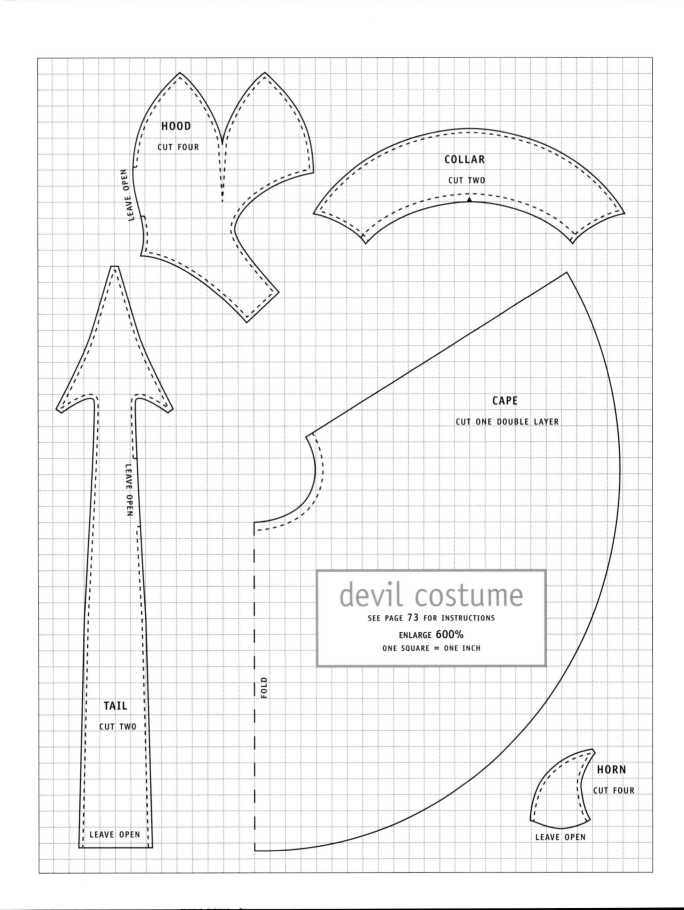

HOOD
CUT FOUR

LEAVE OPEN

COLLAR
CUT TWO

CAPE
CUT ONE DOUBLE LAYER

LEAVE OPEN

FOLD

devil costume
SEE PAGE 73 FOR INSTRUCTIONS
ENLARGE 600%
ONE SQUARE = ONE INCH

TAIL
CUT TWO

LEAVE OPEN

HORN
CUT FOUR

LEAVE OPEN

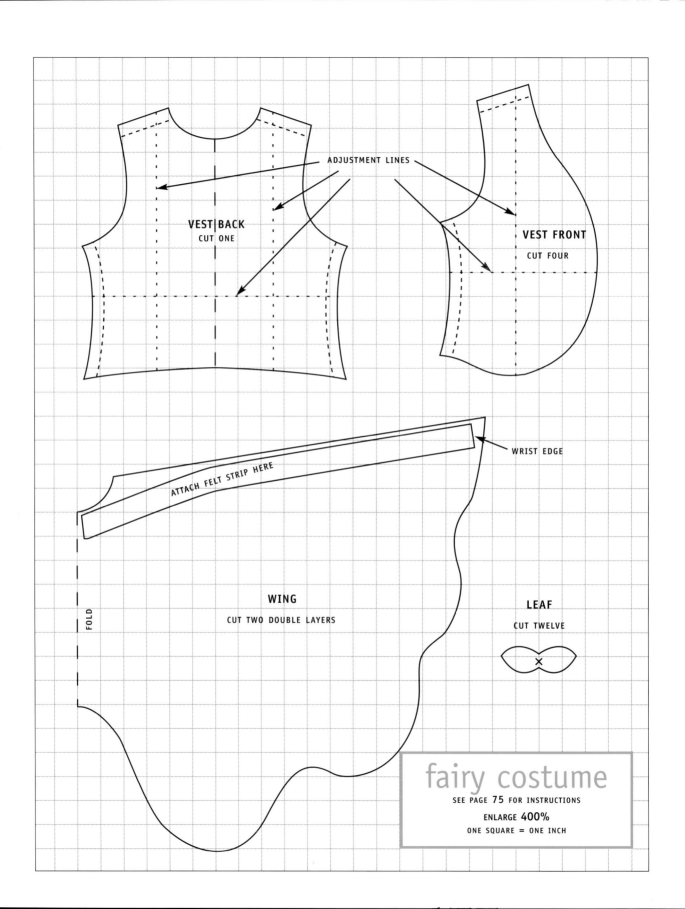

ADJUSTMENT LINES

VEST BACK
CUT ONE

VEST FRONT
CUT FOUR

WRIST EDGE

ATTACH FELT STRIP HERE

FOLD

WING
CUT TWO DOUBLE LAYERS

LEAF
CUT TWELVE

fairy costume
SEE PAGE **75** FOR INSTRUCTIONS
ENLARGE **400%**
ONE SQUARE = ONE INCH

skeleton costume

SEE PAGE **81** FOR INSTRUCTIONS

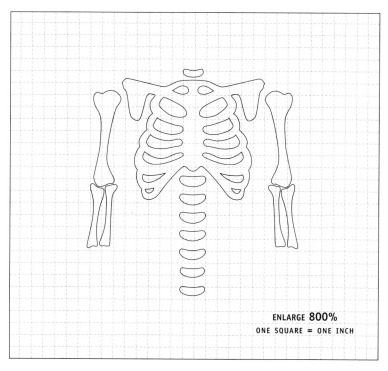

ENLARGE 800%
ONE SQUARE = ONE INCH

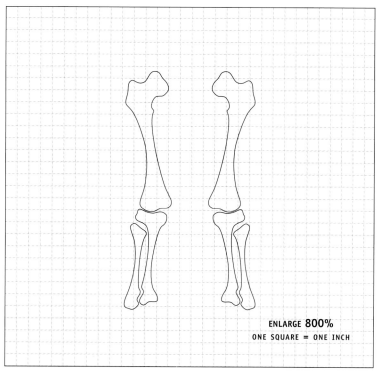

ENLARGE 800%
ONE SQUARE = ONE INCH

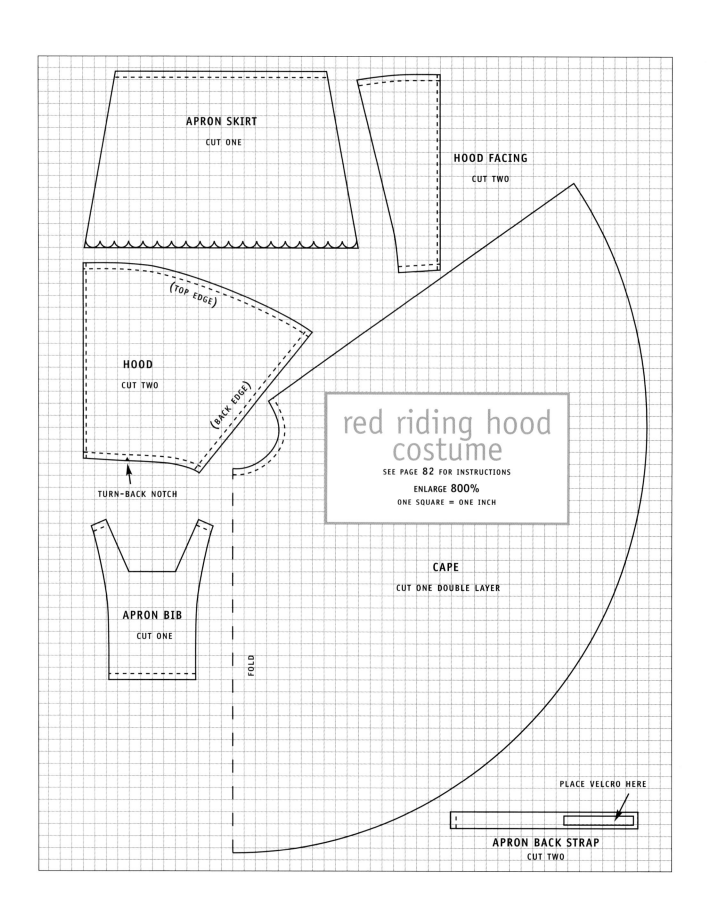

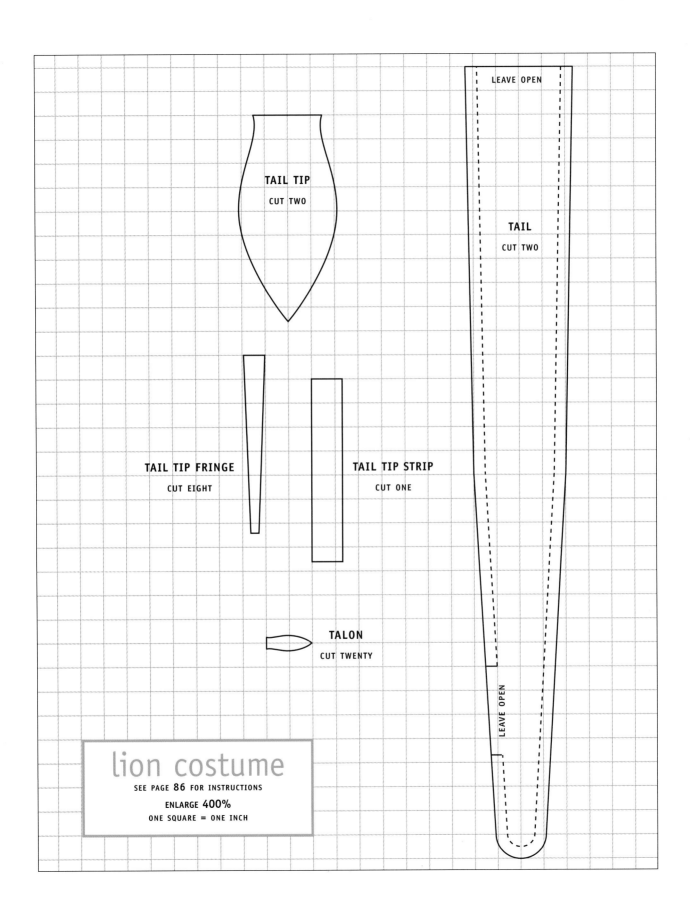

TAIL TIP

CUT TWO

TAIL

CUT TWO

LEAVE OPEN

TAIL TIP FRINGE

CUT EIGHT

TAIL TIP STRIP

CUT ONE

TALON

CUT TWENTY

LEAVE OPEN

lion costume

SEE PAGE **86** FOR INSTRUCTIONS

ENLARGE **400%**

ONE SQUARE = ONE INCH

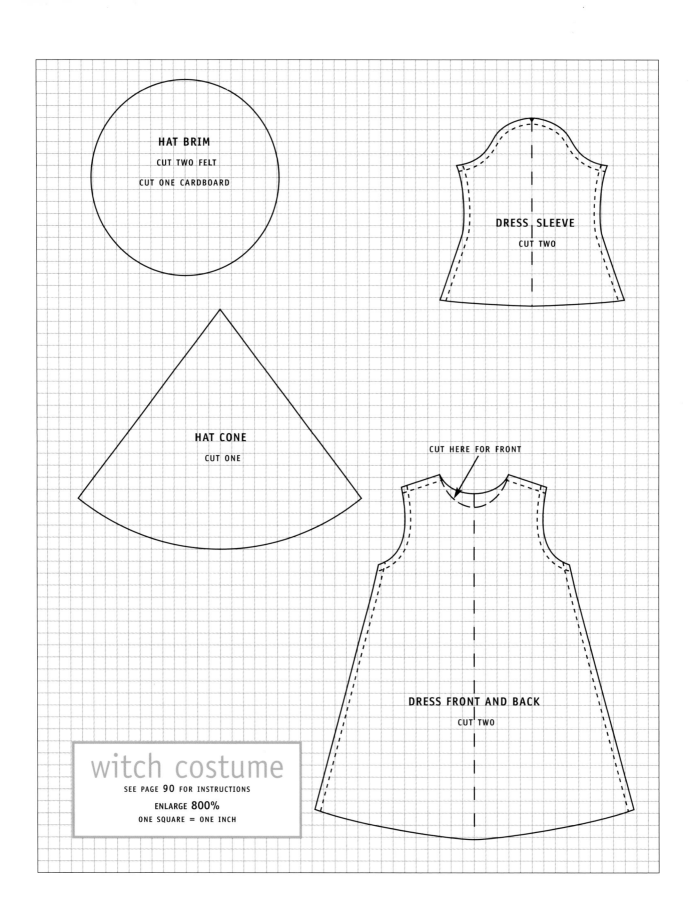

HAT BRIM
CUT TWO FELT
CUT ONE CARDBOARD

DRESS SLEEVE
CUT TWO

HAT CONE
CUT ONE

CUT HERE FOR FRONT

DRESS FRONT AND BACK
CUT TWO

witch costume
SEE PAGE 90 FOR INSTRUCTIONS
ENLARGE 800%
ONE SQUARE = ONE INCH

index